LEISURE ARTS PRESENTS

THE SPIRIT OF CHRISTMAS

CREATIVE HOLIDAY IDEAS
BOOK ONE

We celebrate each Christmas for only a short time, yet the feelings and experiences we share during the holiday season can be a joy forever. These feelings are reflected in the sparkling and colorful decorations that make our holiday homes more beautiful and inviting. They are embodied in the presents that are created with care and given with love. And they are nourished by the holiday food and hospitality that is shared with family and friends. The plans in this book are designed to enhance the joy of the holidays for you and your loved ones. Here you'll discover enchanting decorations to craft for your home. You'll find easy-to-make gifts that are all the more precious because they express the love in your heart. You'll taste the excitement and holiday cheer of festive meals and delicious treats for your guests. The sights, the sharing, and the tastes of Christmas — all these cherished aspects of the holidays reflect the warm and generous spirit of the season. This spirit of Christmas goodwill comes from within ourselves, as we give of ourselves. And this is the spirit we want to share with you, now and for all the holidays to come.

RIVERWOOD PRESS
A Division of Leisure Arts, Inc.
Little Rock, Arkansas

THE SPIRIT OF CHRISTMAS

"...and it was always said of him, that he knew how to keep Christmas well, if any man alive possessed the knowledge. May that be truly said of us, and all of us!"

— From *A Christmas Carol* by Charles Dickens

EDITORIAL STAFF

Editor-in-Chief: Anne Van Wagner Young
Managing Editor: Sandra Graham Case
Art Director: Gloria Hodgson
Assistant Editor: Susan Frantz Wiles
Production Director: Jane Kenner Hoffman
Production Assistant — Decorating, Gifts, and Food: Micah McConnell
Production Assistant — Decorating, Gifts, and Food: Paula Henshaw Moyer
Production Assistant — Food: Kay Wright
Production Artist: Linda Lovette Fraim
Assistant Production Artist: Leslie Loring Krebs
Copy Assistants: Carla Clift Bentley, Jana Beauchamp Fee, Yanna Jo Lamb Hester, and Darla Burdette Kelsay
Typesetters: Laura Glover Burris and Tracy Stanley Evans
Contributing Editor: Arlin Fields

BUSINESS STAFF

Executive Director of Marketing and Circulation: Steven B. Weintz
Controller: Tom Siebenmorgen
Retail Sales Director: Richard Tignor
Retail Marketing Director: Pam Stebbins
Retail Customer Services Director: Margaret Sweetin
Marketing Manager: Russ Barnett
Printing and Distribution Manager: Joe Buhajla
Circulation Manager: Marsha M. Hriz
Publisher: Steve Patterson

THE SPIRIT OF CHRISTMAS
Creative Holiday Ideas, Book One

Copyright© 1987 by Riverwood Press
104 Riverwood Road
North Little Rock, Arkansas 72118

Printed in the United States of America.
First Printing.

International Standard Book Number
0-942237-00-5

TABLE OF CONTENTS

REFLECTIONS OF THE HOLIDAY 74

THE SHARING OF CHRISTMAS . . 86

THE SPIRIT OF CHRISTMAS

TABLE OF CONTENTS

(Continued)

THE TASTES OF CHRISTMAS.120

CHRISTMAS COOKIE KLATCH 122

A FESTIVE FAMILY DINNER 132

MERRY COUNTRY BRUNCH ...140

HOLIDAY OPEN HOUSE 148

GENERAL INSTRUCTIONS 157

CREDITS 159

THE SIGHTS
OF·CHRISTMAS

*The sights of Christmas give the season its sparkle, and home
is where the holiday spirit shines brightest. Festive trimmings all
through the house set a cheerful mood when family and
friends gather to share the joys of the season.
In this section, we bring you six collections of decorations
to fill your home with the spirit of Christmas. Within each
theme, you'll find coordinated projects to make your home beautiful
and inviting, as well as to trim your tree and your packages. You
can use all of the ideas in a collection, or you can choose just a few
to give a fresh look to your traditional decorations.
Your family will have "A Beary Merry Christmas" when you
decorate with lots of lovable, huggable teddy bears. Folk art creations
made of homespun and twigs will bring you a charming pioneer
"Christmas on the Prairie." To craft "A Natural Celebration,"
you can decorate with the season's favorite fruits and spices. There's
a Victorian influence in the nostalgic "Romance and Roses"
collection. Old World images of Santa dominate a Christmas
"Among the Pines and Vines." Or if you're always dreaming of
a white Christmas, you can design a winter wonderland
with the "Reflections of the Holiday" projects.
Invite the spirit of Christmas into your home with handmade
decorations that reflect the holiday mood you choose to create.
You'll add a sparkle to the season that will shine forever in the
hearts and memories of those you love!*

Lovable, huggable teddy bears can be the start of your merriest Christmas ever. Between the bears you already have and the ones we'll help you make, you can fill your home with decorations that warm the heart.

Christmas is a time for renewing old friendships, and the treasured teddy bears that you've collected through the years are a lot like old friends — you've hugged them close and shared your deepest secrets with them. Now you can let them join in your holiday fun. Your favorite bear can have the honor of playing Santa, while the others can trim your tree and greet your guests. Whether you have one bear or 50, let them capture the joy of the season — for your children, and for the child in you!

Our projects are shown in detail on the next five pages, and the instructions begin on page 15. Enjoy a Beary Merry Christmas at your house this year!

A Beary Merry Christmas begins at the door with trimmings that set a playful holiday mood. Teddy isn't quite finished decorating this **Door Wreath and Garland** *(page 17)*, so Reindeer Bear has rounded up a wagonload of helpers. It won't be long now before all the greenery is dotted with bows and bears that were made ahead of time. The bright fabric bows are crafted of draping fabric that has been formed into bows and painted. The stuffed fabric bears are made with the pattern for our Teddy Bear String; Christmas print fabrics make them extra festive.

Waiting for Santa can be lots of fun when you cuddle up with your favorite bears. The hours will pass in a twinkling, and suddenly you'll turn to find that Santa Bear has arrived — and that he's delighted to find his picture on your **Bear Sweater** *(page 16)*! Making this cozy top is easy: just follow our instructions for using waste canvas to cross stitch the design on a purchased sweater. We chose a midnight blue sweater to give the design the nighttime setting that Santa prefers for his travels.

On the night before Christmas, girls and boys everywhere will be hanging their stockings by the chimney with care. The lucky ones will have our special **Bear Stocking** *(page 19)* to hold Santa's deliveries. Its snowscape and teddy bear Santa (laden with sticks for the naughty and toys for the nice!) are appliquéd onto a stocking that you make with our pattern. The name is added with a gold glitter pen.

The perfect task for a basket is holding special gifts and accessories. Our **Bear Basket** *(page 16)* is holding potpourri sachets and fabric bears like those in the **Teddy Bear String** *(page 17)* that is draped across the back of the chair.

Brown craft paper is the main ingredient in this **Santa Bear Garland** *(page 19)*. All you do is fanfold the paper, make a few simple cuts, and then paint each Santa's coat and hat. The garland will stand on its own wherever you want a touch of Christmas, or you can drape it across a wall or on a tree.

Gifts that are lovingly chosen or handmade deserve special packaging. Our **Gift Wraps** *(page 15)* are a quick and inexpensive answer. The printed wrapping paper is made by stamping brown craft paper with a potato carving that's coated with paint. The gift bags are created with plain brown lunch sacks. Our **Tree Skirt** *(page 15)* provides a simple background for these festive packages.

Small stuffed bears create a circle of love in this **Teddy Bear Wreath** *(page 17)*. The tiny packages propped at each side are **Potpourri Sachets** *(page 19)* filled with a fresh woodsy scent.

If teddy bears could sing, our Noel quartet would be humming a Christmas carol. To make this charming arrangement, dress up your bears with satin bows or collars of ruffled eyelet. Seat them casually and let them hold wooden letters that have been spray-painted a glossy red. Holly provides the finishing touch.

Santa Bear *(page 18)* is making a list and checking it twice — he knows who's been naughty or nice! Your favorite bear can have the honor of playing Santa, too. Just cut a fleecy beard, sew a felt hat, and bend some gold wire into eyeglasses for him. Then prop him up in a little chair and put a ledger in his lap. Your calligraphy skills will come in handy to help Santa list all the good and bad little bears in your family.

Reindeer Bear *(page 18)*, sporting felt antlers and a red pom-pom nose, is resting up for his Christmas Eve ride with Santa. Parked outdoors to greet your guests and charm passers-by, he loves his job of watching over some of the gifts for that special delivery. Those with handmade gift wraps are his favorites, and he's giving special attention to a little package bearing printed wrapping paper.

Need a ''bearutiful'' centerpiece that's bursting with Christmas cheer? Wrap a gift box with pretty paper or fabric, line it with tissue paper, and set a stuffed bear inside. Add a couple of stuffed fabric bears that you make with our Teddy Bear String pattern and top everything off with a tiny package, a big bow, and a sprig of holly. Your bear-in-a-box is ready to wish everyone a Beary Merry Christmas!

FABRIC BOWS

(Shown on pages 10 and 12.)

You will need craft draping fabric, gesso, red gloss enamel spray paint, white acrylic paint, small paintbrush, and waxed paper.

(**Note:** Fabric bows are made using a craft draping fabric. The fabric contains glue that is activated when misted with water. This craft draping fabric is available at craft stores.)
1. To make each bow, you will need fabric strips cut in these sizes:
    Tree Bow: 8½" x 24½" for bow loops and 3½" x 4" for binding strip.
    Treetop Bow: 25" x 40" for bow loops and 7" x 9" for binding strip.
2. For binding strip, mist fabric on both sides with water. (**Note:** It is important for the fabric to become flexible, but it should not become limp. If this should happen, allow fabric to dry until it becomes manageable.) Fold each long edge to center, overlapping edges ¼" (**Fig. 1**); press with fingers to flatten. Set aside.

Fig. 1

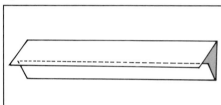

3. For bow loops, follow Step 2 to mist and fold fabric. Place short ends together, overlapping ¼" to form a circle. (**Note:** Be sure smooth side is on the outside.) With overlap in back, gather center, forming two loops (**Fig. 2**). Place crumpled waxed paper inside bow loops to keep them from sticking together.

Fig. 2

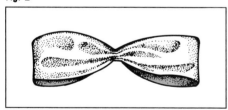

4. Some bows were made with streamers as shown on pages 8 and 9. For streamers, cut one strip of craft draping fabric 8½" x 36" and follow Step 2 to mist and fold fabric. Keeping smooth side down, fold each end at a 45° angle; press with fingers to flatten. Place center of streamers behind bow loops.
5. Wrap binding strip, smooth side out, tightly over gathered area of bow loops (and streamers, if used). Leaving a ½" overlap in back, cut off excess. Set bow aside and allow to dry.
6. Coat bow with gesso on front and back; allow to dry. (**Note:** Gesso may cause bow to relax slightly, but bow will retain its shape and reharden when dry.)
7. Paint bow using red enamel spray paint. It may be necessary to use more than one coat to get an even coverage. Let dry thoroughly between coats. If desired, polka dots may be painted on bow using white acrylic paint.

GIFT WRAPS (Shown on page 12.)

For each Gift Bag, you will need a brown paper lunch sack, 2⅞"w plaid craft ribbon, Creative Twist™ or heavy twine, brown gummed tape, craft glue, and tracing paper.

1. Trace bear pattern onto tracing paper and cut out.
2. Pin pattern on ribbon; cut out.
3. Cut 3" from top of paper bag.
4. Fold top edge 1" to inside of bag.
5. For handles, cut two 13" lengths of Creative Twist™ or heavy twine. Position one length on inside front of bag with ends approx. 1" from sides. Secure with a 4" piece of gummed tape. Repeat for back of bag.
6. Referring to photo for placement, glue bear to bag.
(**Note:** Colored tissue paper and ribbon may be used to add a special finishing touch to your gift bag.)

For Printed Wrapping Paper, you will need a potato that is large enough to accommodate pattern, brown or plaid craft paper, craft knife, tracing paper, desired color acrylic paint, paper towels, and 1"w paintbrush.

1. Trace bear or heart pattern onto tracing paper and cut out.
2. Cut potato in half lengthwise. You will use one half of potato for each pattern.
3. Lay pattern on flat side of potato. Using a craft knife, cut into potato ¼" as you cut around pattern. Leaving design raised ¼" for stamping, remove potato around pattern.
4. Brush a thin layer of desired color acrylic paint on raised portion of potato. Press potato onto paper towel to remove excess paint. You may wish to practice transferring design onto a piece of paper to determine the amount of paint needed to produce a good transfer.
5. Using a stamping motion, transfer design to craft paper.
(**Note:** Packages may be tied with jute or accented with craft ribbon.)

BEAR

HEART

TREE SKIRT (Shown on page 12.)

For a 40" diameter skirt, you will need 1¼ yds of red felt, 3⅝ yds of ⅝" dia. white ball fringe, thumbtack or pin, pencil, and string.

1. Fold a 45" x 45" piece of felt in half from top to bottom and again from left to right.
2. To mark outer cutting line, tie one end of a 25" length of string to a pencil. Insert thumbtack or pin through string 20" from pencil. Insert tack in felt as shown in **Fig. 1**, and mark one-fourth of a circle.
3. To mark a 4" dia. inner cutting line, repeat Step 2 using 2" of string between pencil and thumbtack or pin. Mark one-fourth of a circle.
4. Following cutting lines and cutting through all thicknesses, cut out skirt. For slit in back of skirt, cut along one fold from outer edge to inner cutting line.
5. Sew ball fringe to outer edge.

Fig. 1

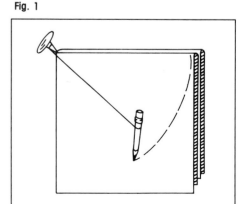

BEAR BASKET (Shown on page 12.)

(**Note:** This is **NOT** a toy for young children as it is constructed with wires and could be dangerous.)

You will need a basket, stuffed bear, heavy wire or coat hanger, wire cutters, hot glue gun, glue sticks, and ribbon to trim bear and basket (optional). **For bear's hat,** you will need a 15" x 17" piece of red felt, 6" x 15½" piece of white fake fur, red and white thread, 7" of ¼"w elastic, and one ⅝" dia. white shank button.

(**Note:** Instructions are for an 18" high stuffed bear. Adjust length of wires to fit your bear.)
1. Cut off each hind leg 2½" from bottom of foot. Cut two 7" pieces of wire and bend in half until ends of wire are approx. 2" apart. Insert folded end of each wire in center of leg as shown in **Fig. 1**, leaving ends of wire extending 1" from leg. Glue opening closed.

Fig. 1

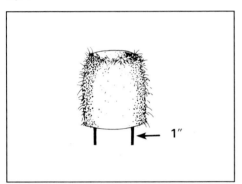

2. Cut off body approx. 1" below upper legs. Cut a 12" piece of wire and bend in half until ends of wire are approx. 5" apart. Insert folded end of wire in center of body as shown in **Fig. 2**, leaving ends of wire extending 2" from body. Glue opening closed.

Fig. 2

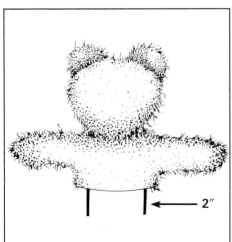

3. Centering body piece at one end of basket, insert wires into rim of basket; glue to secure. Position feet as desired at other end of basket and insert wires into rim of basket; glue to secure. If desired, trim bear and basket with ribbon.
4. For bear's hat, follow Steps 5 — 8 of Santa Bear, page 18.

BEAR SWEATER (Shown on page 11.)

(38w x 58h)

Fig. 1

Fig. 2

Fig. 3

You will need a sweater; 8.5 count waste canvas; lightweight, non-fusible interfacing; 8" dia. screw-type hoop; #24 Tapestry needle; embroidery floss (see color key); masking tape, and tweezers.

1. Cut waste canvas 8½" x 11"; cover edges of canvas with masking tape. To provide a firm stitching base, cut a piece of interfacing the same size as canvas.
2. To mark center of design on sweater, fold sweater in half lengthwise. Measure along folded edge desired number of inches from neck to center of design; mark with a pin.
3. Match center of canvas to pin. Use the blue threads in canvas to place canvas straight on sweater; pin canvas to sweater. Pin interfacing to wrong side of sweater. Baste all three thicknesses together as shown in **Fig. 1**.
4. Place sweater in a screw-type hoop. We recommend a hoop that is large enough to encircle entire design. Roll excess fabric, including back of sweater, over top edge of hoop; pin in place (**Fig. 2**).
5. Using a #24 Tapestry needle, work design using 6 strands of floss for Cross Stitch, 2 for Backstitch, and 4 for French Knots. Stitch from large holes to large holes.
6. Trim canvas to within ¾" of design. Dampen canvas until it becomes limp. Pull out canvas threads one at a time using tweezers (**Fig. 3**).
7. Trim interfacing close to design.

X	DMC	B'ST	ANC.	COLOR
⊙	ecru		0926	ecru
	310	☑	0403	black
✳	321		047	lt red
V	436		0365	tan
	437		0362	lt tan
◐	498		019	red
✕	699		0923	green
◆	703		0238	lt green
+	761		08	pink
★	815		044	dk red
△	822		0390	beige
▬	911		0205	dk green
●	310		black French Knot	

Design size using 8.5 count waste canvas - 4½" x 6⅞".

TEDDY BEAR STRING

(Shown on page 12.)

You will need twelve 8" squares of desired fabric, tracing paper, fabric marking pencil, thread to match fabric, polyester fiberfill, small crochet hook, black embroidery floss, and 1⅓ yds of 1"w satin ribbon.

1. Use pattern on this page and follow **Transferring Patterns** and **Sewing Shapes**, page 157, to make six bears.
2. Turn bears right side out and stuff with fiberfill. Sew final closure by hand. Hand stitch through all thicknesses along dashed lines on bears' ears.
3. Using black embroidery floss, satin stitch eyes and noses and outline stitch mouths. (**Note:** When stitching facial features, knot floss and enter head through seam line. Hide knot by giving floss a small tug to pop knot through to the inside. Stitch features and exit through seam line.)
4. Referring to photo for placement, whipstitch bears together.
5. Cut two 4" lengths and two 20" lengths of ribbon. Whipstitch one end of a 4" length of ribbon to each end of Teddy Bear String. Tie two remaining lengths of ribbon in bows. Whipstitch a bow to the end of each ribbon.

DOOR WREATH AND GARLAND (Shown on page 10.)

You will need an artificial evergreen wreath and garland to fit your door, one Treetop Bow with polka dots and two Tree Bows with polka dots (see Fabric Bows, page 15), desired number of individual stuffed fabric bears (see Steps 1 – 3 of Teddy Bear String on this page), and green florist wire.

1. Referring to photo, wire Treetop Bow and stuffed fabric bears to wreath.
2. Referring to photo, wire Tree Bows and stuffed fabric bears to garland.

TEDDY BEAR WREATH

(Shown on page 13.)

You will need an artificial evergreen wreath (we used a 26" dia. wreath); stuffed bear to fit inside of wreath (we used a 12" bear); small stuffed bears (we used 4" bears); blue glass ball ornaments; ⅛"w, ¼"w, and ⅝"w red satin ribbon; craft glue; green florist wire; white acrylic paint, and small paintbrush to paint ribbons (optional).

1. If desired, paint polka dots on some of the ribbons using acrylic paint. Allow to dry.
2. Using ⅝"w ribbon, tie a bow around large bear's neck. Referring to photo for placement, wire bear to inside of wreath. Tack hanger of one glass ball ornament to bear's paw.
3. Using ⅛"w ribbon, tie a bow around each small bear's neck. Referring to photo for placement of bears, place wire around each small bear's neck and use wire to attach bears to wreath. Wire glass ball ornaments to wreath.
4. Referring to photo, place ¼"w ribbon on wreath; glue to secure.

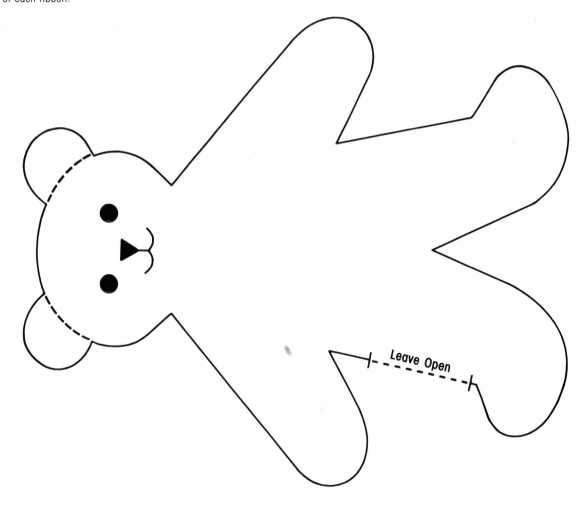

Leave Open

SANTA BEAR (Shown on page 13.)

You will need a stuffed bear, 8" square of shearling fabric (artificial lambswool), tracing paper, craft glue, 22" of gold wire, 2" strip of Velcro® fastener, 15" x 17" piece of red felt, red and white thread, 6" x 15½" piece of white fake fur, 7" of ¼"w elastic, and one ⅝" dia. white shank button.

(**Note:** Instructions are for an approx. 18" high stuffed bear. Adjust beard, hat, and glasses to fit your bear.)
1. For beard pattern, use pattern on this page and follow **Transferring Patterns**, page 157.
2. Pin pattern to wrong side of shearling fabric; cut out, cutting through backing only.
3. Cut two 1" lengths of Velcro® fastener. (**Note:** You will only need the hook or firm side.) Glue Velcro® fastener to wrong side of beard at upper corners. Referring to photo, place beard on bear.
4. For glasses, refer to photo for shape and bend wire as shown in **Fig. 1** to fit bear's face. Hook ends of wire behind ears.

Fig. 1

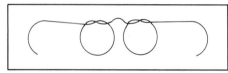

5. For hat, fold felt in half lengthwise. Sew a diagonal seam from one folded corner to opposite outer corner. Leaving approx. ¼" seam allowance, trim excess fabric. Turn right side out.
6. (**Note:** Use ¼" seam allowance throughout.) For cuff, match right sides of fur and sew short edges together. With right sides facing, place cuff over hat matching raw edges and seams; sew pieces together. Turn cuff right side out. With wrong sides together, fold cuff in half. Turn raw edge of cuff under ¼" and whipstitch to seam allowance.
7. For neck strap, center seam in back and tack each end of elastic to inside of cuff on sides of hat.
8. Sew button to point of hat.

REINDEER BEAR (Shown on page 14.)

You will need a stuffed bear, four 5" x 7" pieces of tan felt, tan thread, polyester fiberfill, tracing paper, water-soluble fabric marking pen, two 4" lengths of heavy wire, 1" dia. red pom-pom, 18" of ⅛"w black elastic cording, 25" of ⅞"w red satin ribbon, white acrylic paint, and small paintbrush.

(**Note:** Instructions are for an approx. 18" high stuffed bear. Adjust pattern to fit your bear.)
1. For antlers, trace pattern on this page onto tracing paper and cut out.
2. Draw around pattern on one piece of felt using water-soluble fabric marking pen.
3. With two pieces of felt together, sew directly on pen line, leaving bottom open for stuffing. Repeat for second antler.
4. Leaving approx. ⅛" seam allowance, cut out antlers. Remove marking pen lines following manufacturer's instructions.
5. Lightly stuff each antler with polyester fiberfill and insert one wire into each antler. Sew final closure by hand.
6. Referring to photo for placement, securely tack antlers to back of ears and head.

7. For pom-pom nose, thread black elastic cording through pom-pom, centering pom-pom on elastic. Tie ends of elastic together in a double knot. Slip elastic over head so pom-pom covers bear's nose.
8. If desired, paint polka dots on ribbon using acrylic paint. Allow to dry. Tie bow around bear's neck.

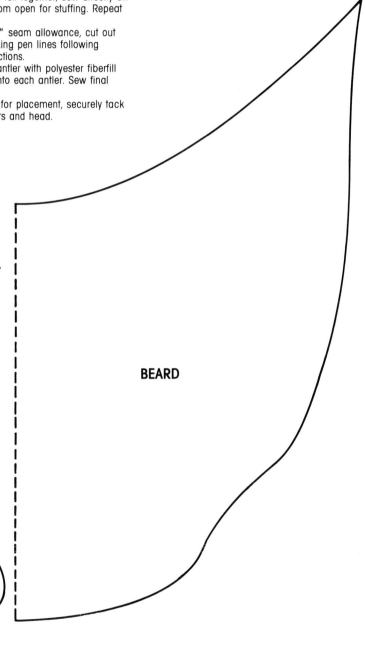

Leave Open

ANTLER

BEARD

SANTA BEAR GARLAND (Shown on page 12.)

You will need brown craft paper (4"h and desired length), tracing paper, transfer paper, red and white acrylic paint, small paintbrush, small stencil brush or cotton swab, paper towels, and black permanent felt-tip pen.

1. For first pleat, lightly draw a line 2¼" from one short edge of paper. Fold on line.
2. Turn paper over. Using first pleat as a guide, fanfold to end of strip.
3. Trace pattern, including dashed lines on hands and coat, onto tracing paper and cut out.
4. Placing dashed lines at folded edges of paper, draw around pattern on first pleat.
5. Being careful not to cut at dashed lines and cutting through all pleats, cut out garland.
6. Unfold paper and lay it flat. Using pattern and transfer paper, transfer coats and hats to garland. Paint coats and hats with red acrylic paint. Allow to dry.
7. Dip dry stencil brush or cotton swab into white acrylic paint. Blot excess onto paper towel. Using a straight up-and-down motion, dab on paint to create a furry effect for beard, and coat and hat trims. Allow to dry.
8. Referring to pattern, use pen to draw facial features.

Place on fold of paper

Place on fold of paper

POTPOURRI SACHETS
(Shown on page 12.)

For potpourri, you will need ¼ cup red rose petals, ½ cup patchouli leaves, ¼ cup pine needles (cut into small pieces), ¼ cup cedar shavings, 1 oz. powdered orrisroot, 9 drops of patchouli oil, glass jar with tight-fitting lid, and four sachets (instructions below).
For each sachet, you will need two 4" x 4" pieces of desired fabric, thread to match fabric, and 24" of ribbon.

1. Mix ingredients for potpourri and place in jar. Secure lid on jar. Place jar in a cool, dark, dry place for two weeks. Every few days, shake jar to mix contents.
2. To make each sachet, place right sides together. Using ½" seam allowance and leaving an opening for turning, sew fabric pieces together. Trim seams and cut corners diagonally. Turn right side out.
3. Fill with potpourri and sew final closure by hand.
4. Tie sachet with ribbon to resemble a package.

BEAR STOCKING (Shown on page 11.)

You will need ½ yd of navy pin-dot fabric; 1 yd of red corduroy fabric; 12" x 14" piece of white felt; small pieces of green fabric, yellow fabric, and tan felt; 3" x 4" piece of burlap (one 4" side should be on selvage); 8" of 3-ply jute; thread to match fabrics and brown thread for sticks; ½ yd of fusible interfacing; ¼ yd of fusible webbing; reusable pressing sheet (available at fabric stores for use with fusible webbing); 2 gold sequin stars; 2 gold seed beads; approx. 18 white seed beads; one ¼" dia. white pom-pom; craft glue; tracing paper; black embroidery floss; small amount of polyester fiberfill; miniature toys, and gold glitter pen.

(**Note:** When instructions indicate machine appliqué, use a narrow zigzag stitch and a short stitch length.)
1. For Stocking pattern (pages 20 and 21), trace thick lines of entire Stocking pattern onto tracing paper, beginning with Cuff pattern and matching arrows and ▲'s; cut out. With navy pin-dot fabric folded in half and cutting through both thicknesses, cut out front and back of Stocking. With red corduroy folded in half and cutting through both thicknesses, cut out front and back of Stocking lining. With fusible side of interfacing up, cut out one Stocking.
2. Trace Cuff pattern, page 20, onto tracing paper and cut out. Fold red corduroy and place pattern on fold as indicated; cut out Cuff. Repeat for second Cuff.
3. Using white felt, cut a 1" x 13" piece for cuff trim.
4. Referring to photo for position of front of Stocking (toe is facing left) and using front Stocking piece of navy pin-dot fabric, fuse interfacing to wrong side of fabric.
5. Trace Bottom Of Stocking pattern, page 20, onto tracing paper and cut out. Using fusible webbing and pressing sheet (follow manufacturer's instructions), fuse webbing to one

side of an 8" x 11" piece of white felt. Pin pattern on right side of felt and cut out Bottom Of Stocking. With webbed side down, fuse Bottom Of Stocking to front of Stocking. Machine appliqué across top edge of Bottom Of Stocking.
6. Trace the following pattern pieces, page 21, onto tracing paper along solid and dashed lines: body (use thick black lines), ears, hat trim, face (use grey dashed lines only), beard, hands, feet, coat trim, tree, and moon. Cut out pattern pieces.
Note: Refer to pattern for placement of all pieces in Steps 7 – 12.
7. Follow instructions in Step 5 to fuse webbing to wrong side of the following fabrics: red corduroy for body; tan felt for ears, feet, and hands. Pin patterns on right sides of fabrics and cut out shapes. Fuse shapes to Stocking and machine appliqué outer edges, including lines for sleeves on body.
8. Pin patterns on the following fabrics and cut out shapes: tan felt for face; white felt for hat trim, beard, and coat trim. Glue shapes to Stocking (do not machine appliqué) in the following order: face, hat trim, beard, and coat trim. Allow to dry.
9. Follow instructions in Step 5 to fuse webbing to wrong side of green fabric for tree and yellow fabric for moon. Pin patterns on right sides of fabrics and cut out shapes. Fuse shapes to Stocking and machine appliqué outer edges.
10. For sticks, it is easier to create your own arrangement than to duplicate pattern exactly. Using brown thread, machine appliqué sticks.
11. Secure each sequin star to Stocking with one gold seed bead. Sew white seed beads to tree.
12. Using 6 strands of black embroidery floss, work French Knots for facial features.
13. (**Note:** Use ¼" seam allowance throughout.) With right sides facing and leaving top edge open, sew front and back of Stocking together; repeat for lining. Trim seams and clip curves. Turn Stocking (not lining) right side out.
14. With right sides facing, sew sides of Cuff

pieces together to form a continuous loop. With wrong sides together, fold Cuff in half lengthwise and match raw edges.
15. Placing Cuff over Stocking and matching raw edges and seams, sew pieces together. Fold top edge ¼" to inside.
16. With wrong sides together, insert lining into Stocking. Fold top edge of lining ½" to wrong side and pin to Stocking.
17. For hanger, cut a 2½" x 4" piece from red corduroy. With right sides together, fold in half lengthwise and sew long edges together. Trim seam and turn right side out. Fold hanger in half matching raw edges. Place raw edges of hanger between lining and Stocking at right seam line; pin in place with approx. 1" extending above Stocking.
18. Slipstitch lining to Stocking and, at the same time, securely sew hanger in place.
19. For cuff trim, glue white felt piece under Cuff, with ½" of felt extending below Cuff.
20. For toy bag, fold burlap piece in half with short sides together. With selvage edge at top and using ½" seam allowance, sew side edge and bottom edge. Trim seams and turn right side out. Using one ply of 3-ply jute and beginning and ending at side seam, make a running stitch ½" from top edge. Lightly stuff bag with fiberfill. Pull jute to slightly gather bag; tie ends of jute together in a knot. Glue miniature toys in opening of bag. Referring to photo for placement of bag, thread ends of jute through front of Stocking where indicated on pattern. Secure ends on inside of Stocking and trim. Glue or tack bottom of bag to Stocking.
21. Glue white pom-pom to hat trim where indicated on pattern.
22. Using gold glitter pen, write name at bottom of Stocking.

Patterns are on pages 20 and 21.

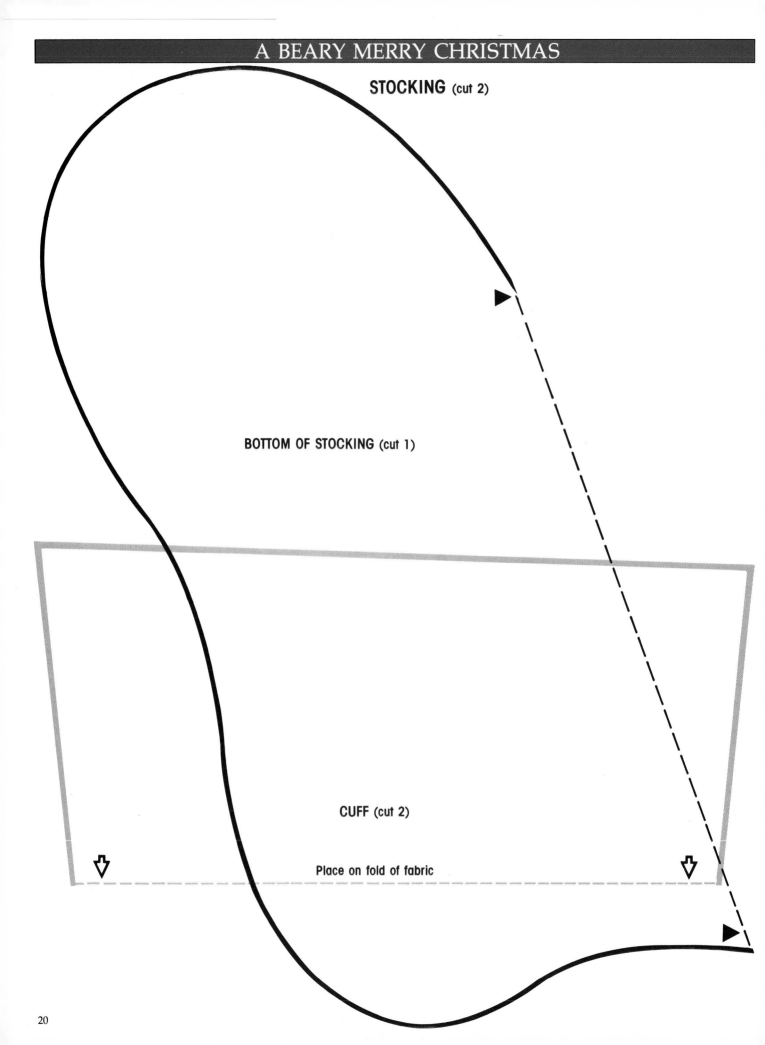

STOCKING (cut 2)

BOTTOM OF STOCKING (cut 1)

CUFF (cut 2)

Place on fold of fabric

Pattern Key

◖ pom-pom
★ star
• white seed bead
● black French Knot
✛ thread jute through fabric

In the early days on the American prairie, time and talent were more plentiful than money and materials. Access to ready-made goods was limited, and it often took a long trip or a long wait to receive supplies. Not to be defeated, the prairie folk crafted their holiday decorations and gifts from the materials at hand. The results were folk art creations that were humble in origin but rich in imagination and love.

In our ''Christmas on the Prairie'' collection, we step back in time to the pioneer Christmases of the past to recapture the homey charm. Everyday items like twigs and fabric scraps are transformed into star and rag ball ornaments. There are prairie-style angels and Santas that reflect our American heritage, and even a primitive Nativity scene set in a tiny twig stable.

Instructions for the projects in this collection begin on page 29. Let the spirit of a prairie Christmas enrich your holiday celebration this year.

Commonplace twigs become something special when you use them to make these simple **Twig Stars** *(page 35)*. The larger ones look especially heavenly when you hang an angel in the center.

Our **Prairie Tree** *(page 33)*, which is shown in full on page 23, is made by adding artificial branches to a real tree trunk. Its branches are trimmed with a big collection of folk art ornaments. **Prairie Angels** *(page 29)* and **Twig Stars** *(page 35)* symbolize the religious nature of the holiday, while **Prairie Santas** *(page 29)* and **Reindeer** *(page 30)* represent some of our favorite legendary Christmas figures. The quilted hearts are one of three styles of **Sugar Cookie Ornaments** *(page 35)*. Each of the **Rag Ball Ornaments** *(page 33)* has a Styrofoam® ball at its core so the wrapping goes quickly. Little **Puffy Hearts** *(page 33)* are miniature versions of the big **Treetop Heart** *(page 33)* that is shown on page 23. Raffia bows and candles complete the trimmings. Underneath it all, a plump cat motif decorates the ruffled homespun **Prairie Tree Skirt** *(page 35)*, while cats and hearts cut from fabric scraps dress up the **Gift Wraps** *(page 30)*.

These **Merry Christmas Blocks** *(page 35)*, cut from an ordinary two-by-four, spell warm wishes for the holiday. Candles in Christmas colors add to their charm when you drill holes in the tops of some of the blocks. **Wooden Trees** *(page 31)* with a wintry look make the warmth of this Christmas message glow even more cheerfully.

The warm glow of candlelight and the sweet look of heart cookies make our **Feather Tree Centerpiece** *(page 31)* simply charming. From the angel at the top to the colorful rag balls holding the candles, this little tree will fill your heart with Christmas cheer.

A sampling of prairie-style ornaments makes a charming holiday arrangement for an entry hall table. After that special gathering of family and friends, delight your guests by letting each of them choose an ornament to take home.

A friendly herd of **Reindeer** *(page 30)*, snug in their winter fur, finds shelter among our wooden trees. The patterns for these dear animals come in four sizes so you can make a whole family of them to help you celebrate Christmas.

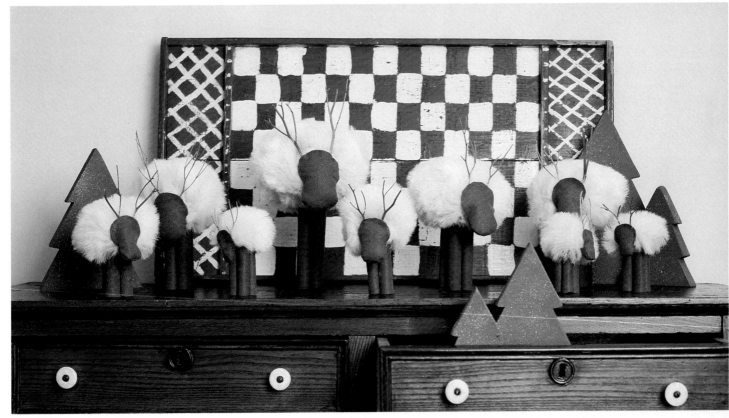

A primitive twig stable is the perfect backdrop for this tiny **Prairie Nativity** *(page 32)*. The scene, complete with kneeling sheep, recalls the humble setting of the birth of Jesus.

The frugal prairie folk would be proud of you for making this **Poster Board Santa Quilt** *(page 34)*. It's easy to create this unique wall or door decoration with only a few simple supplies. You just cut poster board into the specified shapes, glue the pieces in place, and paint the areas by shape. Staining gives it an antiqued look.

Just as the cook always saves her best aprons for special occasions, you can use our little **Apron Garland** *(page 31)* during the holidays to add a cheerful touch to a rustic setting. For a sweet accent, set out a bowl of decorated cookies made according to the instructions for our **Sugar Cookie Ornaments** *(page 35)*. The festive bows on the cats capture the joy of the season, while the fabric-covered hearts are reminiscent of an old custom that European immigrants brought to America: they decorated their holiday cookies with colorful pictures that could be peeled off and saved as mementos before the cookies were eaten. What a tasty tradition!

Place a batch of **Apple Potpourri** *(page 30)* on a side table and watch the faces of everyone who walks past — the spicy aroma of this colorful concoction will have them all looking for holiday baked goods. It's the kind of scent that makes you close your eyes, breathe deeply, and dream of apple pie and sumptuous cakes.

PRAIRIE ANGELS (Shown on page 24.)

For each angel, you will need two 5" squares of desired fabric for dress; two 3" squares of muslin for head; two 3" x 4" pieces of muslin for wings; tracing paper; fabric marking pencil; small crochet hook; polyester fiberfill; Spanish moss; thread to match fabric and moss; black, brown, and rose embroidery floss; 7" of jute; craft glue; cosmetic blush, and nylon line for hanger.

1. Use head and dress/coat patterns and follow **Tranferring Patterns** and **Sewing Shapes**, page 157, to make one head from muslin and one dress from desired fabric.
2. Fold opening in dress ¼" to wrong side and press. Stuff head and dress with fiberfill. Insert neck of head into opening in dress and whipstitch head to dress.
3. For facial features, use 2 strands of floss and enter head through seam line. Work black French Knots for eyes and rose Straight Stitch for mouth; exit through seam line. Blush cheeks.
4. For hair, use 6 strands of brown floss and work French Knots along seam line where indicated by ●'s on pattern.
5. For wings, sew 3" x 4" muslin pieces together, using ¼" seam allowance and leaving an opening for turning. Turn right side out and sew final closure by hand. Fold wings in half matching short edges and press with fingers to mark center. Work basting stitch through both thicknesses along fold line in center of wings; pull thread to slightly gather. Referring to photo and centering wings on back of dress, tack wings to dress and head.
6. For halo, twist a small amount of Spanish moss together to form a 1½" dia. ring. Wrap thread around moss to secure halo. Refer to photo and glue halo to head.
7. Tie jute in a bow and glue to neck.
8. For hanger, thread 8" of nylon line through top of angel and knot ends of line together.

PRAIRIE SANTAS (Shown on page 24.)

For each Santa, you will need three 5" squares of desired fabric for coat and hat, two 3" squares of muslin for head, tracing paper, fabric marking pencil, small crochet hook, polyester fiberfill, thread to match fabric, cotton batting, scrap piece of white felt, small twig, black and rose embroidery floss, craft glue, cosmetic blush, and nylon line for hanger.

1. Use head and dress/coat patterns and follow **Transferring Patterns** and **Sewing Shapes**, page 157, to make one head from muslin and one coat from desired fabric.
2. Follow Steps 2 and 3 of Prairie Angels instructions to finish head and coat and to work facial features.
3. For hat, trace pattern onto tracing paper and cut out. Use fabric marking pencil to draw around pattern on wrong side of remaining 5" square of fabric; cut out. Overlap long edges of hat as indicated by dashed line on pattern; glue in place. Referring to photo and with seam in back, glue hat on head. Fold point of hat down and glue or tack in place.
4. Cut cotton batting ¼"w x 4"l for hat trim and ¾"w x 8"l for coat trim. Referring to photo for placement, glue trims in place.
5. Referring to photo, glue fiberfill to point of hat and to face to form beard.
6. For mittens, trace pattern onto tracing paper and cut out. Use pattern and cut out two mittens from white felt. Referring to photo for position of twig and mittens, glue twig and mittens to coat.
7. For hanger, thread 8" of nylon line through top of Santa and knot ends of line together.

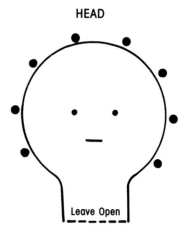

HEAD

Leave Open

(Note: French Knot hair as indicated by ●'s is for Prairie Angel only.)

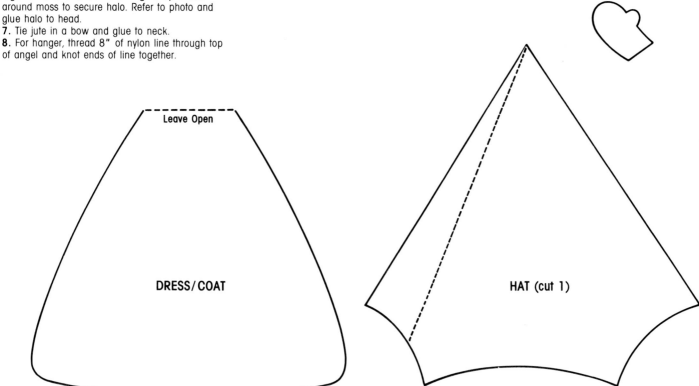

MITTEN (cut 2)

Leave Open

DRESS/COAT

HAT (cut 1)

REINDEER (Shown on page 26.)

You will need fake fur, brown felt, heavy thread (buttonhole twist), polyester fiberfill, small twigs for antlers, hot glue gun, glue sticks, and nylon line for hanger.

1. For desired size reindeer, use the following measurements for cutting out pieces (cut through backing of fur only):
   Small reindeer: 3" dia. circle of fake fur for body, four 3" x 7" pieces of felt for legs, and a 2½" x 3½" piece of felt for head.
   Medium reindeer: 5½" dia. circle of fake fur for body, four 3½" x 10" pieces of felt for legs, and a 3" x 4½" piece of felt for head.
   Large reindeer: 8" dia. circle of fake fur for body, four 5½" x 12" pieces of felt for legs, and a 3½" x 5½" piece of felt for head.
   Extra large reindeer: 11" dia. circle of fake fur for body, four 6" x 13" pieces of felt for legs, and a 4" x 6½" piece of felt for head.
2. For each leg, begin at one short edge of felt and roll piece tightly together; glue edge to secure roll. Repeat to make a total of four legs. Keeping ends of rolls even and seams to the inside, glue rolls together.
3. For body, use a double strand of heavy thread and baste around fur ¼" from edge. Pull ends of thread to gather body slightly. Lightly stuff with fiberfill. Insert legs ½" into opening in body and add more fiberfill if necessary. Pull ends of thread to gather body tightly around legs. Knot thread and trim ends. Glue body to legs.
4. For head, trace pattern onto tracing paper and cut out. Use pattern and cut out one head from felt. Reusing pattern, cut out lower part of head (grey area). Matching edges, whipstitch outer edges of head pieces together. Turn right side out and stuff with fiberfill.
5. For antlers, glue one end of twigs to wrong side of head where indicated on pattern by **X**'s. Refer to photo for position and glue head to body.
6. For hanger on small reindeer, thread 8" of nylon line through top center of body and knot ends of line together.

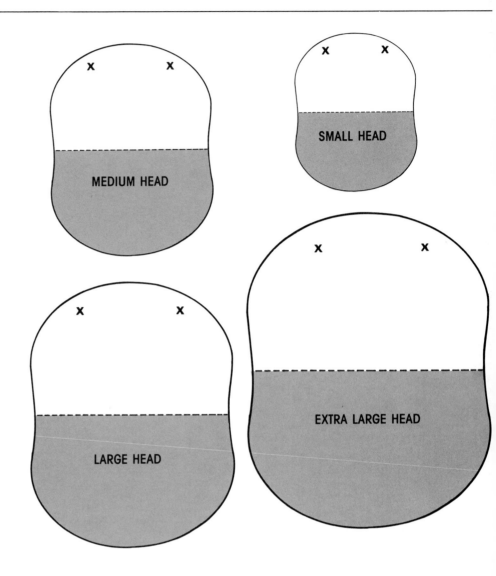

GIFT WRAPS (Shown on page 24.)

You will need fabric or brown craft paper, raffia, strips of fabric, tracing paper, scraps of fabric for cutouts, medium-weight paper for gift tags, craft glue, fabric marking pencil, and black permanent felt-tip pen with fine point.

1. Wrap packages with brown craft paper or fabric.
2. Tie packages with raffia or fabric strips torn in desired lengths and widths.
3. For fabric heart trim, trace desired heart pattern on this page onto tracing paper and cut out. For cat trim, use smallest cat pattern on page 35 and follow **Transferring Patterns**, page 157.
4. Use fabric marking pencil to draw around pattern on wrong side of fabric; cut out shape.
5. For gift tag, use medium-weight paper and cut tag large enough to accommodate desired shape.
6. Glue shape to package or gift tag. Use felt-tip pen to draw dashed line around shape to resemble quilting.

APPLE POTPOURRI

(Shown on page 28.)

You will need 1 cup dried apple slices (see Dried Fruit Ornaments, page 44; omit acrylic spray and hangers), 2 tablespoons ground cinnamon, ¼ cup whole allspice berries, approx. 10 two-inch long cinnamon sticks, 2 tablespoons whole cloves, ¼ cup canella or nandina berries, approx. 10 small pinecones, 7 drops of cinnamon oil, glass jar with tight-fitting lid, and decorative non-metal container to hold potpourri.

1. Mix ingredients for potpourri and place in jar. Secure lid on jar. Place jar in a cool, dark, dry place for two weeks. Every few days, shake jar to mix contents. (**Note:** Cinnamon oil has an extremely strong scent that intensifies as it absorbs into the potpourri. Additional oil may be added as needed.)
2. Place potpourri in container. Additional dried apple slices may be added to accent potpourri.

FEATHER TREE CENTERPIECE

(Shown on page 25.)

You will need a small feather tree (we used an 18" tree), small block of Styrofoam®, raffia, flat basket or container, desired number of 1½" dia. rag balls (see Rag Ball Ornaments, Step 2, page 33; cover balls with ¼"w fabric strips), craft knife, thin green florist wire, hot glue gun, glue sticks, small birthday-size candles, sugar cookie dough (see Sugar Cookies, page 129), 1"w heart cookie cutter, one angel without hanger (see Prairie Angels, page 29), toothpick, and nylon line to hang cookies.

1. Glue Styrofoam® block to inside of basket. Insert tree into center of foam. Place raffia around base of tree to cover foam.
2. For rag ball candle holders, use craft knife to cut a small hole in each rag ball; insert one candle into hole. Insert wire through a small area of fabric at bottom of each rag ball; use wire to attach ball to branch of tree.
3. For cookie ornaments, roll out dough ¼" thick and use heart cookie cutter to cut out desired number of cookies. Use a toothpick to make a hole for the hanger in the top of each cookie. Bake as directed. For hangers, thread 6" of nylon line through holes in cookies and knot ends of line together. Hang cookies on tree.
4. For treetop angel, insert wire through a small area of fabric on back of angel; use wire to attach angel to top of tree.

APRON GARLAND

(Shown on page 28.)

For each apron, you will need one 6" x 4" piece and one 12" x 1" piece of muslin, thread to match muslin, tracing paper, small square of desired fabric for heart trim, fabric marking pencil, craft glue, and black permanent felt-tip pen with fine point.

1. For apron, fold two short edges and one long edge of 6" x 4" muslin piece ¼" to wrong side; press. Sew close to folded edges. Baste ¼" from raw edge and pull basting threads to slightly gather apron.
2. For apron string, fold each long edge of 12" x 1" muslin piece ¼" to wrong side; press. Fold strip in half lengthwise with wrong sides together and with edges matched; press.
3. Center apron on apron string and insert gathered edge of apron between fold of apron string. Beginning at one end of apron string, sew apron and apron string together.
4. For heart trim, trace heart pattern below onto tracing paper and cut out. Use fabric marking pencil to draw around pattern on wrong side of fabric; cut out heart. Glue heart to corner of apron. Use felt-tip pen to draw dashed line around heart to resemble quilting.
5. Tie desired number of aprons together to form garland.

WOODEN TREES (Shown on page 25.)

For each tree, you will need ½" thick pine lumber (8" x 10" piece for large tree, 6" x 8" piece for medium tree, and 5" x 6" piece for small tree), green and white acrylic paint, 1"w paintbrush, toothbrush, sandpaper, tracing paper, and jigsaw.

1. Use desired size tree pattern and follow Transferring Patterns, page 157.
2. Draw around pattern on wood and use jigsaw to cut out tree. Sand edges.
3. Paint tree with two coats of green acrylic paint.
4. For snow effect, dip toothbrush in white acrylic paint and pull thumb across bristles to spatter paint on tree.

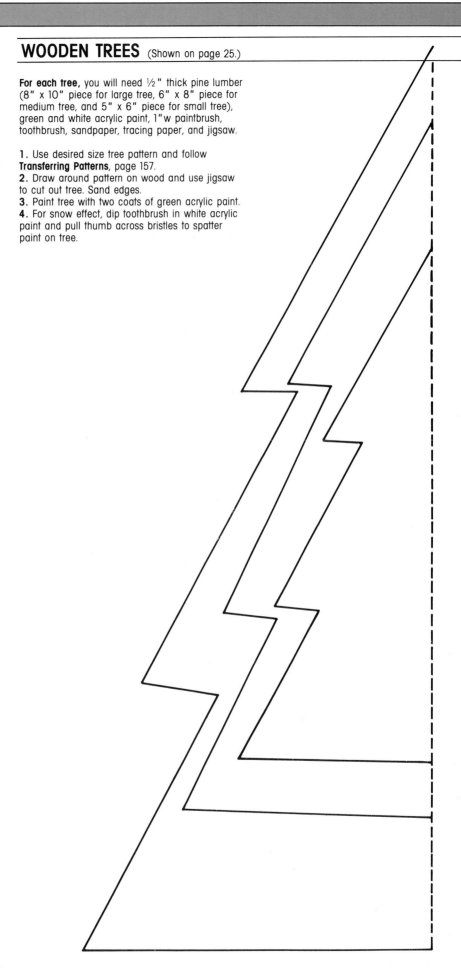

PRAIRIE NATIVITY (Shown on page 27.)

For Mary and Joseph, you will need two 8" squares of muslin for each doll, tracing paper, fabric marking pencil, small crochet hook, polyester fiberfill, popcorn kernels or small dried beans, two 8" squares of desired fabric for each dress, thread to match fabric, one 11½" x 2" piece of felt for Mary's headdress, one 11½" x 2" piece and one 5" x 1" piece of felt for Joseph's headdress, Spanish moss, cosmetic blush, craft glue, and jute.

Dolls

1. Use doll pattern and follow **Transferring Patterns** and **Sewing Shapes**, page 157, to make two dolls from muslin.
2. Fold lower edges ¼" to wrong side; press. For drawstrings, use a double strand of thread and baste along lower edges, leaving 6" ends.
3. Stuff upper sections of dolls with fiberfill as indicated by dashed line on pattern. Use rounded end of crochet hook to stuff fiberfill into small areas. Fill lower sections of dolls with popcorn kernels or small dried beans and pull drawstrings tightly to close; knot and trim ends.
4. Blush cheeks.

Dresses

1. Using dress pattern and sewing shoulder, sleeve, and side seams only, follow **Transferring Patterns** and **Sewing Shapes**, page 157, to make two dresses from desired fabric.
2. Fold bottom edges of dresses ¼" to wrong side; press and sew in place.
3. Fold neck and sleeve openings ¼" to wrong side; press.
4. For neck and sleeve drawstrings, use a double strand of thread. Beginning and ending at back of openings, baste through both layers of fabric. Place dresses on dolls. Pull drawstrings tightly; knot and trim ends.
5. For Joseph's headdress, refer to photo and glue 5" x 1" felt piece to head. Center 11½" x 2" felt piece at top of head. Tie an 8" length of jute around waist to secure headdress.
6. For Joseph's beard, refer to photo and glue Spanish moss to face. For Mary's hair, refer to photo and glue Spanish moss to head.
7. For Mary's headdress, refer to photo and center 11½" x 2" felt piece at top of head. Tie an 8" length of jute around waist to secure headdress.

For Baby Jesus, you will need two 3" squares of muslin, tracing paper, fabric marking pencil, polyester fiberfill, cosmetic blush, craft glue, small crochet hook, and small amount of Spanish moss, and one 5" square of desired fabric for blanket.

1. Using baby pattern and leaving lower edge open, follow **Transferring Patterns** and **Sewing Shapes**, page 157, to make one baby from muslin.
2. Turn lower edge ¼" to wrong side; press.
3. Use rounded end of crochet hook to stuff baby with fiberfill. Sew final closure by hand.
4. For hair, glue a small amount of Spanish moss to head.
5. Blush cheeks.
6. For blanket, fold 5" square of fabric in half to form triangle. Referring to photo, wrap blanket around baby and glue in place.

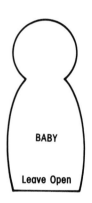

BABY

Leave Open

For each Sheep, you will need one 3" dia. circle of shearling fabric (artificial lambswool), tracing paper, heavy thread (buttonhole twist), polyester fiberfill, craft glue, and one 3" square of black felt.

1. Trace patterns for head and ears onto tracing paper and cut out.
2. Use patterns and cut out head and ears from felt.
3. For body, use a double strand of heavy thread and baste around shearling ¼" from edge. Pull ends of thread to gather body slightly. Stuff body with fiberfill. Pull ends of thread to tightly gather body. Knot thread and trim ends.
4. Referring to photo, glue head and ears to body.

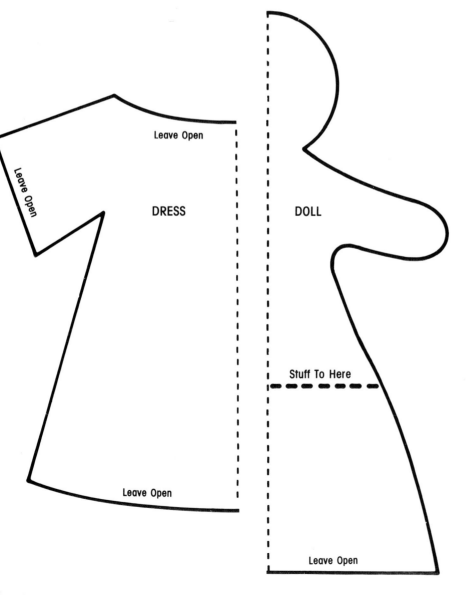

DRESS

Leave Open

Leave Open

Leave Open

DOLL

Stuff To Here

Leave Open

Leave Open

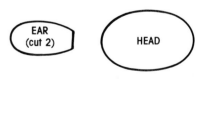

EAR (cut 2)

HEAD

Continued on page 33.

PRAIRIE NATIVITY (continued)

For Twig Stable, you will need twigs approx. ¼" in dia. and smaller, hot glue gun, glue sticks, and Spanish moss.

1. For framework of stable, use larger dia. twigs and follow **Fig. 1** for length and placement; glue twigs in place.

Fig. 1

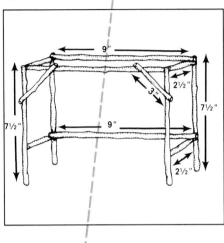

2. For framework of roof, use larger dia. twigs and follow **Fig. 2** for length and placement; glue twigs in place.

Fig. 2

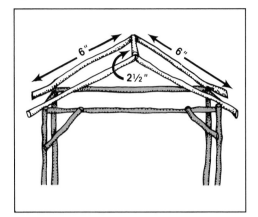

3. For roof top, use 2½" long pieces of smaller dia. twigs and refer to photo for placement; glue twigs in place.
4. For back of stable, lay stable flat with back facing up. Cut larger dia. twigs to fit vertically from roof to lower edge of stable, adjusting lengths as necessary; glue twigs in place.

5. For star, use 2" long pieces of smaller dia. twigs. Referring to photo, glue twigs together to form a five-pointed star; glue star to top of roof.
6. Referring to photo, add Spanish moss to front of stable.
7. For manger, use smaller dia. twigs and follow **Fig. 3** for length and placement; glue twigs in place. Place Spanish moss in manger.

Fig. 3

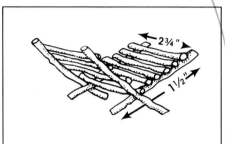

TREETOP HEART (Shown on page 23.)

You will need two 16" squares of homespun or desired fabric, thread to match fabric, polyester fiberfill, tracing paper, thin wire, and fabric marking pencil.

1. Use large heart pattern on this page and follow **Transferring Patterns** and **Sewing Shapes**, page 157, to make one heart.
2. Stuff heart with fiberfill and sew final closure by hand.
3. Insert wire through approx. 2" of fabric on center back of heart; use wire to attach heart to top of tree.

PRAIRIE TREE (Shown on page 23.)

You will need a real tree trunk of desired size (we used a 6' tree), artificial tree branches, tree stand, and electric drill.

1. Remove all branches from tree trunk. Beginning ½" from top of trunk, drill a row of holes around trunk approximately 1" apart. (Holes should be deep and large enough to hold artificial branches.) Drill next row of holes approximately 6" - 8" below first row. Continue for each row of holes, stopping 10" from bottom of trunk.
2. Secure bottom of trunk in tree stand. Graduating sizes, insert branches into holes.

RAG BALL ORNAMENTS

(Shown on page 24.)

For each ball, you will need a 2" or 3"dia. Styrofoam® ball, desired cotton fabric, craft glue, and nylon line for hanger.

1. Tear fabric into 1" wide strips.
2. Glue wrong side of one end of strip to Styrofoam® ball and wrap strip around ball. Overlapping strips, add additional strips as necessary to cover ball. Glue end of last strip to ball.
3. For hanger, thread 8" of nylon line through a small area of fabric on ball and knot ends of line together.

PUFFY HEARTS (Shown on page 24.)

For each heart, you will need two 5" squares of desired fabric, tracing paper, fabric marking pencil, thread to match fabric, polyester fiberfill, small crochet hook, and 8" of jute.

1. Use puffy heart pattern on this page and follow **Transferring Patterns**, page 157.
2. Place fabric pieces right sides together and center pattern on top. Use fabric marking pencil to draw around pattern. **Do not cut out shape.**
3. Fold jute in half and place between fabric pieces with ends extending beyond seam line at top center of heart (looped end will be between fabric pieces). Leaving an opening for turning and stuffing, sew fabric pieces together directly on pencil line, catching ends of jute in seam.

4. Leaving ¼" seam allowance, cut out heart. Clip seam allowance at curves.
5. Turn heart right side out. Use rounded end of crochet hook to completely turn all areas.
6. Stuff lightly with fiberfill. Sew final closure by hand.

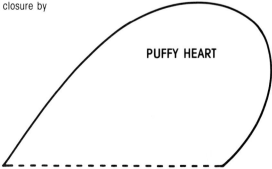

PUFFY HEART

POSTER BOARD SANTA QUILT (Shown on page 27.)

You will need one 22" x 28" piece of white poster board; one 10½" x 27½" piece of heavyweight cardboard; red, black, green, flesh, and white acrylic paint; #6, #10, and 1"w flat paintbrushes; black and red permanent felt-tip pens with fine points; gesso; craft glue; tracing paper; graphite transfer paper; dark fruitwood stain; matte-finish clear acrylic spray; paper towels; soft cloth; sawtooth hanger, and hot glue gun and glue sticks to attach hanger.

1. From poster board, cut one 10½" x 27½" piece, two 1" x 27½" pieces, two 1" x 8½" pieces, and three 6" square pieces.
2. Trace patterns onto tracing paper. Use transfer paper to transfer patterns to poster board; cut out pieces.
3. (**Note:** Before gluing poster board pieces, it may be necessary to thin craft glue with water for even coverage and to avoid ripples and bubbles between layers. While gluing, remove any excess glue from surface with a damp paper towel.) For backing piece, glue the 10½" x 27½" poster board and cardboard pieces together.

4. Referring to diagram for placement, glue the following pieces to the poster board side of backing piece: a 1" x 27½" piece to each long side, a 1" x 8½" piece to each short side, and the 6" square pieces to middle area. Allow to dry.
5. Referring to photo and diagram, glue pieces in the following order: heads, bodies, hat trims, beards, cuffs, belts, and coat trims. Allow to dry.
6. Apply gesso to front of project.
7. Refer to photo and paint as follows:
   Background of backing piece — Green
   1" wide pieces around edges — Red
   Background of 6" squares — White
   Hats and coats — Red
   Faces and hands — Flesh
   Belts and boots — Black
   Hat trims, beards, cuffs, and coat trims — White
8. Referring to pattern for placement, use black pen to draw eyes and red pen to draw mouths.
9. Apply stain to entire project with a soft cloth. Wipe surface to remove excess stain. Allow to dry.
10. Spray entire project with acrylic spray.
11. For hanger, hot glue sawtooth hanger to top center of back.

DIAGRAM

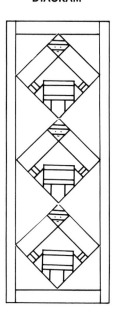

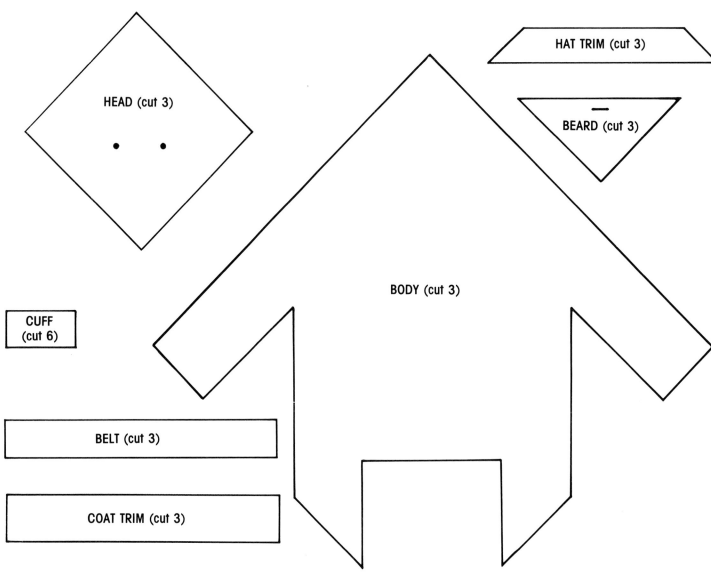

PRAIRIE TREE SKIRT

(Shown on page 24.)

For a 40" diameter skirt, you will need 1¼ yds of 45"w homespun or desired fabric, 3⅜ yds of 2"w pre-gathered muslin ruffle, two 9" squares of muslin for cat trim, fusible webbing, reusable pressing sheet (available at fabric stores for use with fusible webbing), tracing paper, pencil, string, and thumbtack or pin.

1. To make skirt, follow instructions for Tree Skirt, Steps 1 – 4, page 15.
2. For ruffle, turn short ends of ruffle ½" to wrong side and press. With right sides together and matching gathered edge of ruffle to raw edge of skirt, sew ruffle to skirt. Press seam toward skirt.
3. For cat trim, use fusible webbing to fuse muslin squares together. Using fusible webbing and pressing sheet (follow manufacturer's instructions), fuse webbing to one side of fused muslin. Use largest cat pattern on this page and follow **Transferring Patterns**, page 157. Center pattern on muslin square and cut out. With webbed side down, position cat on skirt as desired; fuse cat to skirt.

TWIG STARS (Shown on page 24.)

For each star, you will need five 5", 10", or 15" twigs; raffia; hot glue gun, and glue sticks.

1. Referring to photo if necessary, position twigs to form a five-pointed star; glue points together.
2. Tie two strands of raffia around each point; trim ends.
(**Note:** If desired, hang an angel in center of the 10" or 15" star and tie raffia bow to one point. To make angel, see Prairie Angels, page 29.)

MERRY CHRISTMAS BLOCKS

(Shown on page 25.)

You will need fourteen 3⅝" blocks cut from a 4½' length of two-by-four; red, green, blue, white, gold, grey, and black or desired colors of acrylic paint; 1"w paintbrush; small stencil brush; dark fruitwood stain; sandpaper; 2½" high Roman style lettering stencils; matte-finish clear acrylic spray; soft cloth; candles; ⅞" dia. wood bit, and an electric drill.

1. Sand blocks, rounding edges slightly.
2. For candle holder, drill ⅞" dia. hole ½" deep in center of one side (top) of block; repeat for desired number of blocks.
3. Paint blocks with one coat of grey paint. Allow to dry.
4. Paint blocks desired colors. Allow to dry. For an antiqued look, lightly sand away paint at edges and in several places on blocks .
5. Using black paint, center and stencil "MERRY CHRISTMAS" letters on blocks.
6. Apply stain to blocks with a soft cloth. Wipe surface to remove excess stain. Allow to dry. Spray with acrylic spray.

SUGAR COOKIE ORNAMENTS (Shown on pages 24 and 28.)

You will need sugar cookie dough (see Sugar Cookies, page 129); 3"w and 4"w heart cookie cutters; tracing paper; paring knife and pieces of fabric torn in ¼"w strips for cats; scraps of fabric, fabric marking pencil, 1 cup confectioners' sugar, and 3 tablespoons milk for fabric-covered hearts; toothpick, and nylon line for hangers.

1. **For quilted hearts,** roll out dough ¼" thick and use 3"w heart cookie cutter to cut out desired number of cookies. Use toothpick to make small holes around edge of each cookie to resemble quilting. Use toothpick to make a hole for the hanger in top of each cookie. Bake as directed in recipe. For hangers, thread 8" of nylon line through holes in cookies and knot ends of line together.

2. **For fabric-covered hearts,** use cookie heart pattern and follow **Transferring Patterns**, page 157. Use fabric marking pencil to draw around pattern on wrong side of fabric; cut out desired number of hearts. Roll out dough ¼" thick and use 4"w heart cookie cutter to cut out desired number of cookies. Bake as directed in recipe. For icing, stir confectioners' sugar and milk together. Spread icing over cooled cookies. Place fabric hearts on icing and allow icing to dry.
3. **For cats,** use desired cat pattern and follow **Transferring Patterns**, page 157. Roll out dough ¼" thick and place pattern on dough. Cut around pattern using paring knife for desired number of cookies. Bake as directed in recipe. Tie fabric strips in bows around cats' necks.

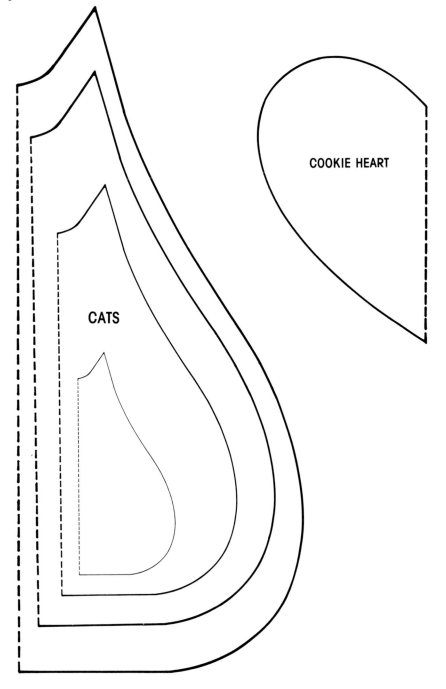

COOKIE HEART

CATS

We often save the best of the fall harvest for special occasions, and it's only natural that part of the bounty should find its way into our holiday decorations. Apples and oranges are traditional Christmas fruits that lend themselves to naturally delightful trimmings. Popcorn and cranberries have inspired generations of families to gather 'round the tree to string garlands of red or white. And the spicy aroma of holiday treats baking in the oven always helps to set a warm and festive mood.

You'll find that the possibilities are endless for crafting beautiful decorations from your cupboard. A stove-top boil of dried fruit and spices fills your holiday home with the scent of Christmas, while popcorn hearts and slices of dried apples and oranges serve as ornaments for your tree. A gingerbread Nativity scene is a natural conversation piece, and an apple stamp leaves a uniquely personal mark on the gifts you wrap.

Instructions for these decorations and more begin on page 42. You'll have your best Christmas ever when you decorate with these delightful accents — because for you, celebrating Christmas comes naturally.

A basketful of Christmas fruits and nuts makes a colorful holiday centerpiece, especially when you add pine needles and some creamy white candles. The fruit virtually arranges itself as it settles into the bed of nuts, making this a quick and easy decoration.

Nothin' says lovin' like somethin' from the oven, and that's where many of these ornaments are made. The **Gingerbread Decorations** *(page 44)* are baked to a golden brown. The **Dried Fruit Ornaments** *(page 44)* start out as juicy slices of apples and oranges. Molded in the shape of an old-fashioned Santa, the **Cinnamon Ornaments** *(page 44)* are oven-dried, too. The **Popcorn Hearts** *(page 47)* are also made in the kitchen — just glue popcorn to both sides of cardboard cutouts. For the finishing touch on your tree, add a garland of fresh cranberries and one of our hand-tied **Creative Twist™ Bows** *(page 43)*.

A plain basket becomes fancy and fragrant when you cover it with cinnamon sticks and add a bit of greenery. We filled our **Cinnamon Stick Potpourri Basket** *(page 47)* with a mixture of dried apples and oranges, allspice berries, and cinnamon stick pieces. When you simmer the potpourri in water, its delicious scent will spread all through the house.

This little village of **Graham Cracker Houses** *(page 43)* is having a white Christmas. The icing that holds the houses together gives them a snowcapped look, while a ready-made lace doily creates a frosty-looking village lawn.

A **Gingerbread Nativity** *(page 42)* provides a natural opportunity for you to share the Christmas story. With an open Bible nearby, you can start the story with scriptures like Isaiah 9:6 that predict Christ's coming, then move on to New Testament accounts of his birth in a lowly stable.

These rustic **Gift Wraps** *(page 44)* will delight your family and friends. The Apple Print Paper is fun to make by using an apple half to stamp paint onto plain paper; the stems and seeds are drawn with a black pen. The Burlap Bags make it easy to wrap your gifts; just tie the bags with jute and trim with **Dried Fruit Ornaments** *(page 44)*, cinnamon sticks, or **Gingerbread Gift Tags** *(page 43)*. Above it all, **Gingerbread Decorations** *(page 44)* look sweet hanging from long ribbons.

Cinnamon sticks, dried fruit slices, and shiny tin molds reflect your holiday decor in this **Natural Wreath** *(page 44)*. Creative Twist™ paper twine adds to the natural charm.

Natural-finish wooden dowels form a tree that you can enjoy year after year, just as Old World families kept small pines that had been stripped of their bark and foliage: each year, the trees were brought out of storage and their branches wrapped with greenery and hung with decorations. We trimmed the limbs of our **Scandinavian Tree** *(page 43)* with Dried Fruit Ornaments, Gingerbread Decorations, and Popcorn Hearts, then topped it with a picture-perfect apple.

Instead of stringing popcorn this year, glue it to cardboard heart cutouts to make this pretty **Popcorn Garland** *(page 46)*. Colorful bows add a festive touch. To make the fruit candle holders, just carve a hole in the top of an apple or orange, making the hole deep enough to support the candle. A bit of greenery can be added to give them holiday flair.

GINGERBREAD NATIVITY (Shown on page 39.)

You will need Gingerbread dough (recipe follows), paring knife, tracing paper, Royal Icing (recipe follows), and pastry decorating bag with small round tip.

GINGERBREAD

- 1 cup butter or margarine
- ¾ cup light brown sugar, firmly packed
- ½ cup sugar
- ⅓ cup molasses
- ¾ cup dark corn syrup
- 3 eggs
- 8½ cups flour
- 1 tablespoon baking soda
- 1 teaspoon salt
- 1 teaspoon allspice
- 1 teaspoon cinnamon
- 1 teaspoon ground cloves
- 1 teaspoon ground ginger

Cream butter and sugars. Add molasses, corn syrup, and eggs. Beat until smooth.

Sift together flour, soda, salt, and spices. Stir into creamed mixture (dough will be stiff).

Divide dough in half and form into two balls. Wrap each half in plastic wrap and chill at least 2 hours.

On lightly floured surface, roll out one half of dough ⅛" thick. Cut out pieces as indicated for projects, using second ball if necessary. Carefully transfer pieces to lightly greased baking sheet. Bake in a preheated 350 degree oven for 8 to 10 minutes or until lightly browned. Place baked pieces on cake rack to cool.

ROYAL ICING

- 3 cups confectioners' sugar
- 2 egg whites

Beat sugar and egg whites together until thick and smooth. Fill pastry bag with icing and cover remaining icing with a damp paper towel to prevent hardening.

NATIVITY

1. Trace patterns on this page onto tracing paper and cut out.

2. Place patterns on dough and cut around patterns using paring knife. (**Note:** Remove any dough scraps and roll into a ball; reserve dough for another use.)

3. For bases, cut one 1" x 3½" piece of dough for Mary, one 1" x 3" piece for Joseph, and one 1" x 1¾" piece for the manger.

4. For stable, cut two 2" x 6" pieces of dough for the roof, two 2" x 6½" pieces for the sides, and one 7½" x 6½" piece for the back.

5. Bake as directed in recipe.

6. Referring to photo and using pastry bag filled with Royal Icing, pipe icing onto one side of stable back to resemble boards. Refer to grey lines on patterns and pipe icing onto Mary, Joseph, and manger pieces. Allow icing to dry thoroughly.

7. Referring to photo, use icing to assemble stable and to attach bases to Mary, Joseph, and manger pieces. Hold pieces in place until icing starts to set; then lay pieces flat until icing dries thoroughly.

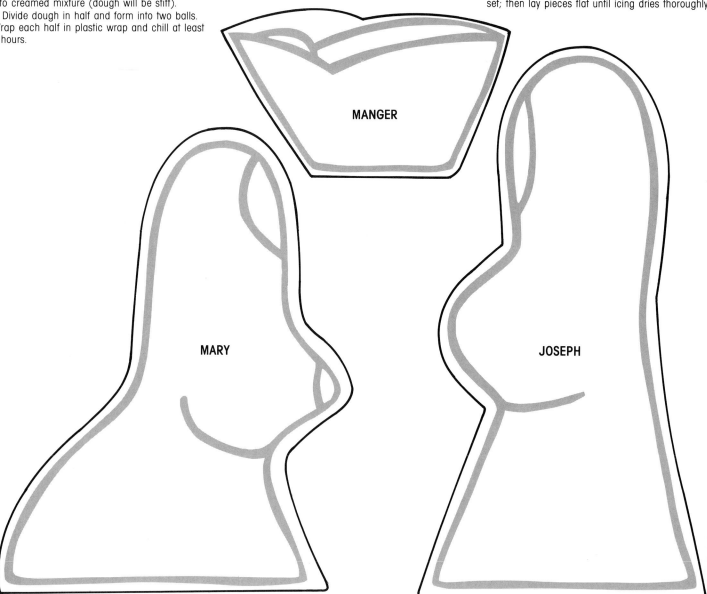

MANGER

MARY

JOSEPH

GRAHAM CRACKER HOUSES (Shown on page 39.)

You will need graham crackers, paring knife, Royal Icing (see Gingerbread Nativity, page 42), and pastry decorating bag with small round tip.

1. For each small house, separate two whole graham crackers into eight pieces along scored lines.
2. To assemble house, pipe icing on long edges of one cracker piece (base). For long sides of house, press long edges of two cracker pieces into icing on base (**Fig. 1**). Hold in place until icing sets.

Fig. 1

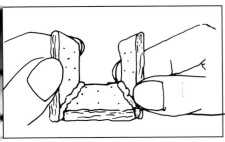

3. For short sides of house, make diagonal cuts for roof points on one short edge of two cracker pieces (**Fig. 2**).

Fig. 2

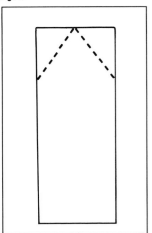

4. Pipe icing on ends of base and short edges of long sides. With pointed ends up, press short sides of house into icing. Hold in place until icing sets.
5. For roof, pipe icing on pointed ends of short sides (**Fig. 3**). Press one cracker piece onto slanted edges on each side to form roof (**Fig. 3**).

Fig. 3

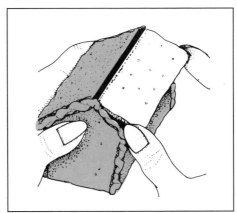

6. For chimney, cut a small rectangle from one cracker piece and pipe icing on one short edge. (**Note:** To place chimney on slant of roof, make diagonal cut on one short edge. Pipe icing on diagonal edge.) Place chimney on roof and hold in place until icing sets.
7. Referring to photo, pipe icing for windows, door, and roof trim.
8. For each large house, separate one whole graham cracker into halves along scored lines (for long sides). Separate two whole graham crackers into eight pieces along scored lines. (**Note:** Only six of the eight cracker pieces will be used.)
9. For long sides of house, cut approx. 1/4" from one edge of each cracker half. Continue with Steps 2 – 6 above. For door, cut one small rectangle from one cracker piece; pipe icing on one long edge. Place door on one long side of house and hold in place until icing sets.
10. Referring to photo, pipe icing for windows and roof trim.

GINGERBREAD GIFT TAGS

(Shown on page 40.)

You will need Gingerbread dough and Royal Icing (see Gingerbread Nativity, page 42), paring knife, drinking straw, pastry decorating bag with small round tip, and jute.

1. Use paring knife to cut dough into desired number of 2" x 3" rectangles. Use straw to make a hole in one corner of each rectangle. Bake as directed in recipe.
2. Using pastry bag filled with Royal Icing, pipe names onto gift tags.
3. Thread 6" of jute through holes in tags and tie tags on packages.

CREATIVE TWIST™ BOWS

(Shown on pages 38 and 40.)

You will need heavyweight Creative Twist™ and florist wire.

1. Cut Creative Twist™ approx. 30" long for treetop bow and approx. 60" long for multi-loop bow on gift package.
2. Untwist Creative Twist™ and tie into desired bow; trim ends. If desired, curl ends around a pencil.
3. Insert wire through back of bow; use wire to attach bow to tree or package.

SCANDINAVIAN TREE

(Shown on page 41.)

For an approx. 25" high tree, you will need one 24 1/2" length of 1/2" dia. dowel; one each of the following lengths of 1/4" dia. dowels: 8", 12", 16" and 20"; one 5" x 7" x 1/2" board; one 7" x 9" x 1/2" board; artificial greenery with wire center; craft glue; electric drill; 1/2" and 1/4" drill bits; one whole apple for top of tree; 6" lengths of nylon line for hanging ornaments; dried apple and orange slices (see Dried Fruit Ornaments, page 44); popcorn hearts (see Popcorn Hearts, page 47), and 3"h or smaller gingerbread cookies in desired shapes (see Gingerbread Decorations, page 44).

1. For tree limbs, mark placement of limbs on 1/2" dia. dowel as shown in **Fig. 1**. Drill 1/4" dia. holes through 1/2" dia. dowel at each mark. Insert 1/4" dia. dowels through 1/2" dia. dowel (**Fig. 1**).

Fig. 1

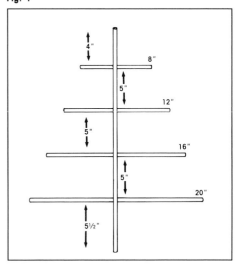

2. For base, center and glue small board to large board. Drill 1/2" dia. hole 1/2" deep in center of small board. Insert tree into base. (**Note:** Tree may be glued together; however, it can be disassembled for storage if glue is not used.)
3. Referring to photo, wrap greenery around tree limbs.
4. Decorate tree with dried apple slices, dried orange slices, popcorn hearts, and gingerbread cookies. Cut a small hole in bottom of whole apple and place apple on top of tree.

DRIED FRUIT ORNAMENTS

(Shown on pages 38 and 40.)

For Dried Orange Slices, you will need oranges, cake racks, clear gloss acrylic spray, and nylon line for hangers.

1. Cut each orange crosswise into ¼" slices; discard end pieces.
2. Place orange slices on cake racks. Dry in oven at 150 degrees or lowest setting for 6 to 8 hours with oven door ajar. (**Note:** Due to variations in individual ovens, check slices occasionally. They should be drying very slowly without turning brown. When dried properly the slices will still be pliable.)
3. Spray slices with acrylic spray.
4. For hangers, thread 8" of nylon line through top of slices and knot ends of line together.

For Dried Apple Slices, you will need apples, lemon juice, salt, citric acid (available in canning section of grocery store), clear gloss acrylic spray, cake racks, and nylon line for hangers.

1. Cut each apple into ¼" slices either crosswise or lengthwise. (**Note:** From each apple cut lengthwise you will get only 3 to 4 slices that contain a portion of the core.)
2. Soak apple slices for 5 minutes in a mixture of 2 cups lemon juice, 3 tablespoons salt, and 3 tablespoons citric acid.
3. To complete project, follow Steps 2 — 4 of Dried Orange Slices.

For Decorated Dried Fruit Ornaments (shown on top of page 40), you will need dried apple slices or dried orange slices, dried greenery, dried flowers, sumac berries, hot glue gun, and glue sticks.

Referring to photo, arrange greenery, flowers, and sumac berries at top of fruit slices; glue in place.

CINNAMON ORNAMENTS

(Shown on page 38.)

You will need cinnamon, applesauce, vegetable oil, desired candy mold (we used a 3"h Santa mold), cake rack, toothpick, and nylon line for hangers.

1. Mix 6 tablespoons warm applesauce and 10 tablespoons cinnamon together to form a ball.
2. Lightly coat mold with oil. Press cinnamon mixture firmly into mold, leveling back; remove ornament from mold. Repeat for desired number of ornaments. Use a toothpick to make a small hole in top of each ornament for hanging.
3. Place ornaments on cake rack. Dry in oven at 150 degrees or lowest setting for 6 to 8 hours with oven door ajar. (**Note:** Due to variations in individual ovens, check ornaments occasionally. They should be drying very slowly.)
4. For hangers, thread 8" of nylon line through top of ornaments and knot ends of line together.

GIFT WRAPS

(Shown on page 40.)

For Apple Print Paper, you will need an apple, newsprint, maroon or desired color acrylic paint, paintbrush, paper towels, jute, and black permanent felt-tip pen.

1. Cut apple in half lengthwise.
2. Brush a thin layer of paint on cut side of apple. Press apple on paper towel to remove excess paint. Use a stamping motion to transfer apple print to paper. Reapply paint to apple as necessary.
3. Referring to photo, draw stems and seeds on apple prints with pen.
4. Wrap packages with apple print paper and tie with jute. Refer to Gift Wrap Trims, listed below, to decorate packages.

For Burlap Bags, you will need burlap, thread to match, and jute.

1. For each bag, cut burlap twice the desired width plus 1" and desired length plus ½" (we cut our bags 13"w x 9"l and 21"w x 12"l).
2. Fold burlap piece in half with short sides together. (**Note:** Folded edge will be on one side.) Using ½" seam allowance, sew along side edge and bottom edge. Turn right side out and fringe top ½".
3. Place gift in bag and tie jute around top of bag. Refer to Gift Wrap Trims, listed below, to decorate bags.

For Gift Wrap Trims, refer to photo and decorate packages and bags as desired with Dried Fruit Ornaments (on this page), Gingerbread Decorations (on this page), Gingerbread Gift Tags (see page 43), Creative Twist™ Bows (see page 43), or cinnamon sticks.

NATURAL WREATH

(Shown on page 40.)

You will need an artificial evergreen wreath (we used a 16" dia. wreath), desired number of dried apple slices (cut crosswise) and dried orange slices (see Dried Fruit Ornaments on this page; omit hangers), 4" long cinnamon sticks (available at kitchen speciality stores), tin molds, medium-weight Creative Twist™ or heavy twine, hot glue gun, and glue sticks.

1. Referring to photo, glue tin molds, cinnamon sticks, and dried fruit slices to wreath.
2. Wrap Creative Twist™ or twine around wreath; glue as necessary to secure.

GINGERBREAD DECORATIONS

(Shown on pages 38 and 40.)

You will need Gingerbread dough (see Gingerbread Nativity, page 42), tracing paper, paring knife, cookie cutters (optional), drinking straw, and ⅝"w grosgrain ribbon or nylon line for hangers.

1. Trace desired patterns on this page and on page 45 onto tracing paper; cut out.
2. Place patterns on dough and cut around patterns using paring knife. (**Note:** If desired, cookie cutters may be used.) **For hand-with-heart cookie,** refer to diagram on page 45 and place heart between thumb and index finger of cookie before baking. Use straw to make a hole for the hanger in top of each cookie. Bake as directed in recipe.
3. For hangers, thread desired lengths of ribbon or 8" of nylon line through holes in cookies and knot ends of line or ribbon together.

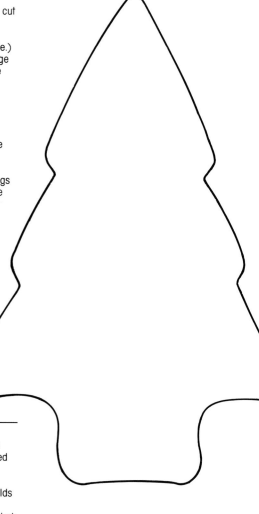

Continued on page 45

44

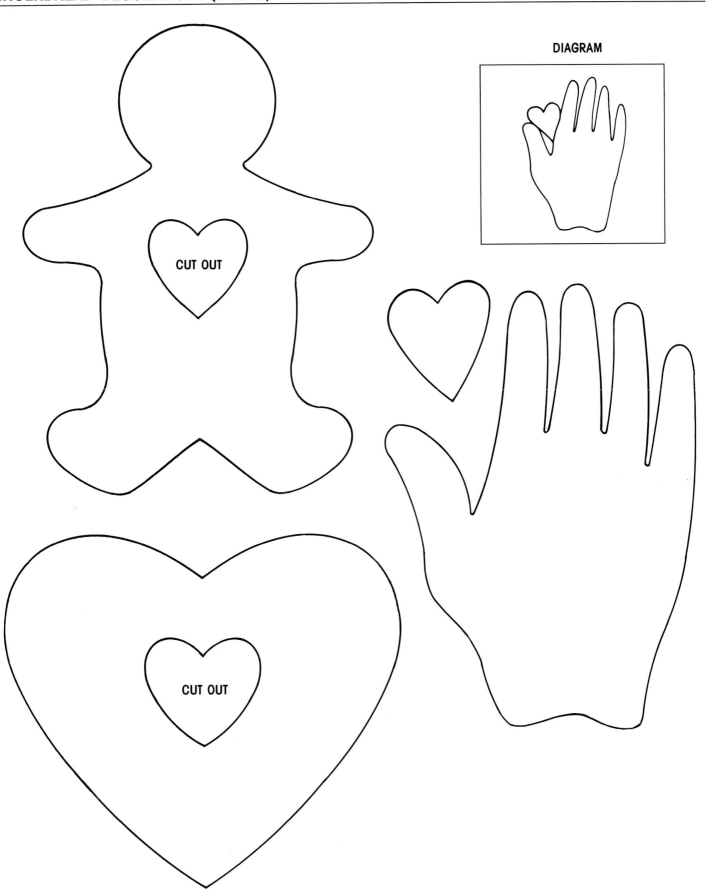

DIAGRAM

CUT OUT

CUT OUT

POPCORN GARLAND (Shown on page 41.)

You will need popped popcorn, one 21" x 17" piece of heavyweight cardboard, tracing paper, utility or craft knife, craft glue, hot glue gun, glue sticks, 14" of 3-ply jute, approx. 4 yds of desired color ⅞"w ribbon, and thread to match ribbon.

1. Use small, medium, and large heart patterns on this page and on page 47. Follow **Transferring Patterns**, page 157.

2. Place patterns on cardboard and draw around 2 small hearts, 2 medium hearts, and one large heart. Use utility or craft knife to cut out hearts.

3. Cover one side of each heart with craft glue and press popcorn into glue. Allow to dry. If needed, glue on more popcorn to fill in any spaces.

4. Cut four 3½" lengths of jute. Refer to **Fig. 1** and place hearts 2½" apart with wrong sides up. Hot glue ends of jute to back of each heart where indicated by **x**'s on patterns.

5. Cut four 22" lengths of ribbon and tie into bows. Center a bow on front of each length of jute; tack in place.

6. Cut remaining ribbon in half. Fold each length in half. Hot glue folded edges of ribbon to back of each small heart at ends of garland.

Fig. 1

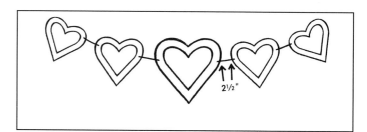

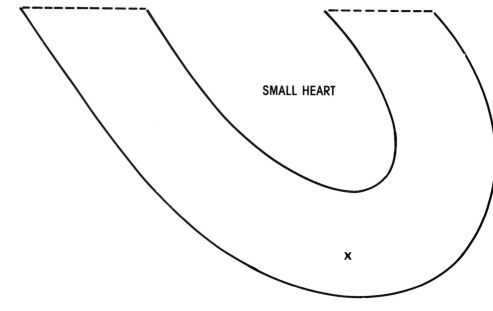

SMALL HEART

x

MEDIUM HEART

x

Continued on page 47.

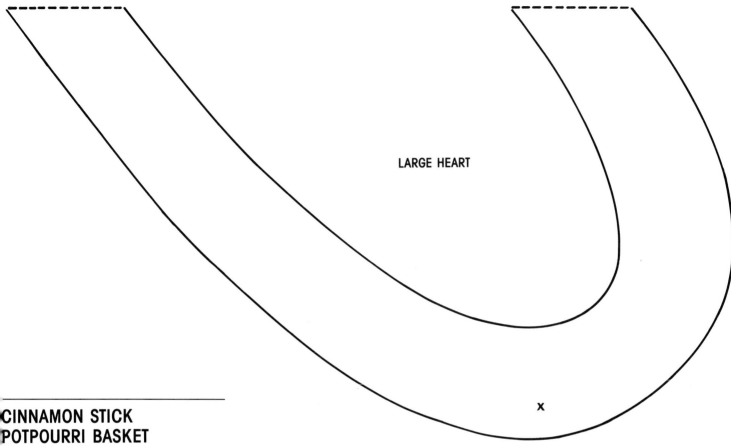

LARGE HEART

x

CINNAMON STICK POTPOURRI BASKET
(Shown on page 39.)

For Cinnamon Potpourri, you will need 1 cup dried orange slices (quartered) and 1 cup dried apple slices (see Dried Fruit Ornaments, page 44; omit acrylic spray and hangers), 1 cup broken cinnamon sticks, ¼ cup allspice berries, 1 teaspoon ground cinnamon, approx. 7 – 9 drops of cinnamon oil, and glass jar with tight-fitting lid.
For Cinnamon Stick Basket, you will need a basket with straight sides (we used a 5" x 3½" market basket stained to match cinnamon sticks), cinnamon sticks, jute, one dried orange slice (see Dried Fruit Ornaments, page 44; omit hanger), dried greenery, dried flowers, hot glue gun, and glue sticks.

1. Mix ingredients for potpourri and place in jar. Secure lid on jar. Place jar in cool, dark, dry place for two weeks. Every few days, shake jar to mix contents.
(**Note:** Cinnamon potpourri may be used as a stove-top boil by mixing ½ cup potpourri with 2 cups water and simmering over low heat.)
2. To make basket, cut cinnamon sticks long enough to extend ¾" above rim of basket. Referring to photo, glue cinnamon sticks around basket.
3. To decorate basket, refer to photo and wrap jute twice around middle of basket; tie at back. Glue greenery, dried flowers, and orange slice to center front of basket.
4. Place potpourri in basket.

POPCORN HEARTS   (Shown on page 38.)

For each heart, you will need popped popcorn, one 3½" square of heavyweight cardboard, utility or craft knife, craft glue, tracing paper, and nylon line for hanger.

1. Trace popcorn heart pattern on this page onto tracing paper and cut out.
2. Place pattern on cardboard and draw around heart. Use utility or craft knife to cut out heart.
3. For hanger, thread 8" of nylon line through center top of heart and knot ends of line together.
4. Cover one side of heart with craft glue and press popcorn into glue. Allow to dry. If necessary, glue on more popcorn to fill in any spaces. Repeat for other side of heart.

POPCORN HEART

V
ictorian times were
an era of elegance and
romance. Lace and flowers
were the favored decorations of
the day, as well as intricate
papercuts, sachets, and
flowing ribbons. Now the
nostalgic charm of a Victorian
holiday celebration can be
yours to share with family
and friends.

Our ''Romance and Roses''
collection takes you back to
those sentimental times with
decorations that smell as
wonderful as they look.
Fragrant potpourri covers
ornaments, a kissing ball, and
a heart-shaped wreath.
Delicate bouquets of dried
flowers add the color of
romance to your tree, which is
elaborately trimmed with paper
roses and a garland of baby's
breath. Colorful birds perch on
the tree's branches, keeping
watch over their nests filled
with golden eggs. With
flowers and lace throughout
the room, there's a feeling of
elegance in the air. Even your
gifts reflect the splendor of the
Victorian setting.

Instructions for these and
other lovely decorations begin
on page 54. (Your local florist
can help you find the dried
materials that make these
projects so special.) This year,
follow your heart and
recapture the elegance and
romance of the Victorian
Christmas!

A garland of white baby's breath, created simply by placing clusters of the delicate flowers side by side, adds a whisper of romance to your tree. **Paper Roses** *(page 59)* are in full bloom, and gold **Papier-Mâché Balls** *(page 59)* reflect the Victorians' love of gilded ornaments. Soft touches of color come from small bouquets of dried red roses, mauve candytuft, asparagus fern, and baby's breath. A string of miniature white lights adds to the elegance.

The elegance of this **Victorian Stocking** *(page 57)* will have everyone thinking it's a prized heirloom. Actually, the technique used to make its lace trim is simple enough for beginners. In no time you'll be finished, and you'll understand why this beautiful lace-making art has been kept alive through the centuries.

The pretty birds on our tree might have laid these golden eggs if we hadn't made them first. Gold spray paint transformed them from ordinary plastic eggs, and a purchased bird's nest provided a natural home for them. Trimmed with a few wisps of dried flowers, this nest of golden eggs makes a pretty tabletop decoration as well as a special trimming for your tree.

Hearts and flowers have always appealed to the sentimental soul, and these crocheted **Heart Motifs** *(page 55)* and **Spanish Moss Baskets** *(page 54)* speak directly to the romantic you. The hearts, designed in three sizes, make lovely decorations or tree ornaments. The baskets, as elegant as they look, are actually simple to make; just glue moss and flowers to the rim of a basket that has been dyed to enhance your choice of flowers.

Bouquets of flowers create an atmosphere of softness that is perfect for a Victorian setting. We used small bouquets all over our tree, then topped it with this big bouquet of the same types of flowers. An elaborate bow of shiny gold ribbon secures our hand-tied arrangement of pepper berries, mauve candytuft, white baby's breath, dried red roses, and asparagus fern. Matching bouquets were placed around the room and were also used to decorate packages.

An ornate **Wreath** *(page 59)*, trimmed in grand fashion with paper roses and shiny gold ribbon, is a splendid example of Victorian style. Balance is achieved with a sprinkling of white baby's breath and pepper berries.

Romance will bloom when you bring out this **Kissing Ball** *(page 54)* covered with sweet-smelling potpourri. And who can resist being captivated by **Scherenschnitte Decorations** *(page 56)* that twirl in the air or adorn a handmade notecard containing a special greeting?

Gathered 'round an evergreen tree symbolizing the eternal life of Christ, these angels sing glory to the newborn King. This delightful papercut is one of three **Scherenschnitte Decorations** *(page 56)* designed to bring the charm of a Victorian Christmas to your home.

The Victorian influence leads to elegant gift wraps. Shimmering moiré fabric makes lovely wrappings, and gold foil paper becomes extra fancy when you spray paint it lightly through a layer of lace (even scraps will do — just overlap the edges slightly). All types of fancy ribbons, cording, and lace can be used to tie the packages, and trimmings can include dried flowers and paper roses.

Invite sweet daydreams of holiday romance by placing bits of fragrance around the room or on your tree. Scented oil gives the **Wax Sachets** *(page 54)* a pleasing perfume, while potpourri brings its own scent to the **Potpourri Balls** *(page 54)*. Both projects are easy ways to create a little elegance.

Our fragrant **Potpourri Wreath** *(page 54)* combines the beauty of lace and flowers to deliver heartfelt holiday greetings to your guests. Its fancy ribbon rosette is a nice touch.

This **Dried Floral Centerpiece** *(page 54)* will have your holiday spirit spiraling upward as your eye follows the rows of flowers that are glued to its cone-shaped base. When you get to the top, there's a red, red rose.

POTPOURRI WREATH

(Shown on page 53.)

You will need one 10"w Styrofoam® heart wreath, potpourri, craft glue, 1 yd of 1"w pre-gathered lace, clusters of pepper berries, 4¼ yds of ¼"w gold metallic ribbon, gold thread, a straight pin, hot glue gun, glue sticks, and ⅛"w satin ribbon for hanger.

1. Working on one section of wreath at a time, cover front and sides of wreath with craft glue and press potpourri firmly into glue. Allow to dry thoroughly. If necessary, glue more potpourri on wreath to cover spaces.
2. Hot glue lace around edge of wreath. Randomly hot glue clusters of pepper berries on top of potpourri.
3. For knotted rosette bow, cut a 3¼ yd length of gold ribbon. Beginning approx. 4½" from one end of ribbon, make 45 knots approx. 2½" apart. Using a double strand of thread and matching knots, take a small stitch in ribbon halfway between each knot (**Fig. 1**). Gather ribbon tightly on thread. Knot thread and trim ends. Referring to photo, hot glue bow to wreath.

Fig. 1

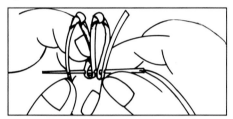

4. Cut remaining length of gold ribbon into five streamers. Referring to photo, hot glue one end of each streamer under bow and secure other ends on top of wreath.
5. For hanger, cut a 6" length of satin ribbon and knot ends of ribbon together. Push pin through knot and dip pin in craft glue. Push pin into back of wreath at top center.

POTPOURRI BALLS

(Shown on page 53.)

For each ball, you will need one 3" dia. Styrofoam® ball, potpourri, craft glue, white baby's breath, ⅛"w burgundy satin ribbon for bow and hanger, and a straight pin.

1. Working on one section of ball at a time, cover ball with craft glue and press potpourri firmly into glue. Allow to dry thoroughly. If necessary, glue more potpourri on ball to cover spaces.
2. Referring to photo, glue baby's breath to top of ball.
3. Using ribbon, make a multi-loop bow. For hanger, cut an 8" length of ribbon and knot ends of ribbon together. Push pin through knot and center of bow; dip pin in glue. Push pin through baby's breath into top of ball.

KISSING BALL (Shown on page 52.)

You will need one 5" dia. Styrofoam® ball, potpourri, craft glue, dried roses, clusters of pepper berries, very small pinecones, candytuft, white baby's breath, purple statice, asparagus fern, ¼"w gold metallic ribbon, a straight pin, hot glue gun, glue sticks, and nylon line for hanger.

1. Follow Step 1 of **Potpourri Balls**, on this page, to cover ball with potpourri.
2. Referring to photo, hot glue an arrangement of fern, baby's breath, statice, candytuft, clusters of pepper berries, pinecones, and roses to top of ball.
3. Make three small bows using gold ribbon. Referring to photo, hot glue bows to arrangement.
4. If hanger is desired, cut a 12" length of nylon line and knot ends of line together. Push pin through knot and dip pin in craft glue. Push pin through arrangement into top of ball.

SPANISH MOSS BASKETS

(Shown on page 51.)

For each basket, you will need a market basket, desired color of fabric dye, Spanish moss, dried white German statice or white baby's breath, dried or silk flowers, a length of 1"w lace that is long enough to go around basket rim, ribbon or cording for bow, hot glue gun, and glue sticks.

1. Mix dye according to package directions and dye basket; allow to dry.
2. Glue lace around basket 1" below rim.
3. Referring to photo, glue Spanish moss to inside and outside of rim (above lace).
4. Referring to photo, glue small pieces of statice or baby's breath in moss; glue flowers in moss.
5. Tie ribbon or cording in a bow and glue to handle at rim.

WAX SACHETS (Shown on page 53.)

For each sachet, you will need paraffin (or pieces of ivory candles), ivory wax coloring chips (if using paraffin), scented oil for candles, candy mold, vegetable oil, double boiler or electric frying pan, large can for melting wax in frying pan, newspapers, craft knife, and ⅛"w satin ribbon for hanger.

1. **CAUTION: Do not melt wax over an open flame or directly on burner.** Cover work area with newspapers. Melt wax over hot water in a double boiler or in a can placed in an electric frying pan filled with water. Add desired number of coloring chips, if using paraffin, and 1 – 2 drops of scented oil.
2. Using vegetable oil, lightly oil mold. Pour melted wax into mold. If hanger is desired, cut a 6" length of ribbon and knot ends of ribbon together. Place knot in wax-filled mold. Allow wax to harden.
3. Remove sachet from mold and trim any uneven edges with craft knife.

DRIED FLORAL CENTERPIECE (Shown on page 53.)

You will need one 18"h Styrofoam® cone, green thread, 2 yds of ¼"w gold metallic ribbon, asparagus fern, white and natural baby's breath, mauve candytuft, clusters of pepper berries, approx. 22 dried red roses, green spray paint, florist or U-pins, straight pins, hot glue gun, and glue sticks.

1. Spray paint cone; allow to dry.
2. Referring to **Fig. 1**, wind thread around cone. Secure ends of thread with straight pins.
3. Using florist pins, attach a row of fern to cone along thread guideline. Referring to diagram, cover cone with alternating rows of candytuft, clusters of pepper berries, and baby's breath.
4. Remove roses from stems. Glue one rose to top of cone. Referring to diagram, glue remaining roses and clusters of pepper berries on top of fern row. If necessary, add more fern to cone to cover spaces.
5. Cut a 15" length of gold ribbon. Referring to diagram, make 3 loops with ribbon. Use a straight pin to pin ribbon in place at top of cone. Pin one end of remaining length of ribbon under loops and

twist loosely around cone. Pin ribbon at base of cone; trim excess.

Fig. 1

DIAGRAM

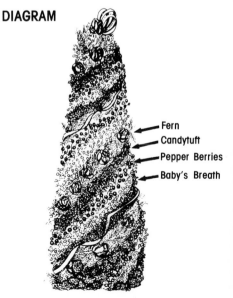

Fern
Candytuft
Pepper Berries
Baby's Breath

HEART MOTIFS (Shown on page 51.)

ABBREVIATIONS

ch(s)	chain(s)
dc	double crochet(s)
mm	millimeters
sc	single crochet
st(s)	stitch(es)
YO	yarn over

( ) or [ ] — work enclosed instructions **as many** times as specified by the number immediately following **or** contains explanatory remarks.

MATERIALS
DMC Cebelia Art. 167/size 10, Ecru
Steel crochet hook, size 7 (1.25 mm) **or** size needed for gauge
GAUGE: 9 dc and 4½ rows = 1"
DO NOT HESITATE TO CHANGE HOOK SIZE TO OBTAIN CORRECT GAUGE.

SMALL HEART

Ch 6 **loosely**.
Row 1: Dc in 4th ch from hook and in remaining 2 chs (**bottom Block made**).
Row 2 (Right side): (Ch 5, turn, dc in 4th ch from hook and in next ch, dc in next dc (**beginning increase made**)), dc in next 2 dc, dc in top of turning ch (turning ch counts as dc now and throughout), work **end Block increase** as follows: (YO, insert hook into base of last dc, pull up a loop, YO, draw through one loop on hook, (YO, draw through 2 loops on hook) twice) 3 times.
Row 3: Work beginning increase, dc in next 3 dc (**Block over Block made**), (ch 2, skip 2 dc, dc in next dc (**Space over Block made**)), work Block over Block, work end Block increase.
Row 4: Work beginning increase, work Block over Block, work Space over Block, (ch 2, dc in next dc (**Space over Space made**)), work Space over Block, work Block over Block, work end Block increase.
Rows 5 and 6: Follow Chart.
Row 7: (Ch 3, turn, dc in next 3 dc (**beginning Block over Block made**)), work 4 Spaces, (work 2 dc in next Space, dc in next dc (**Block over Space made**)), work 4 Spaces, work Block.
Rows 8 and 9: Follow Chart.
First Side — Row 10: Work 5 Blocks.
Row 11: (Turn, slip st in first 4 dc, ch 3 (**beginning decrease made**)), work 3 Blocks; finish off.
Second Side — Row 10: With **right** side facing, join thread with slip st in 3rd dc from First Side, ch 3, work 5 Blocks.
Row 11: Work beginning decrease, work 3 Blocks; do **not** finish off.
EDGING: Ch 6, sc in top of last dc of next row, ch 4, sc in top of middle dc between Sides, ch 4, sc in top of last dc of next row, ch 6, sc in top of last dc of next row, ch 6, skip 4 dc, sc in next dc, ch 6, sc in top of last dc in row, ch 6, sc in top of last dc of next row, ch 6, skip next row, sc in side of next row, ch 6, skip next row, sc in top of last dc of next row, ch 6, sc in top of last dc of next row, continue around in the same manner to beginning ch-6; join with a slip st to first ch, finish off.

MEDIUM HEART

Ch 6 **loosely**.
Row 1: Dc in 4th ch from hook and in remaining 2 chs (**bottom Block made**).
Row 2 (Right side): (Ch 5, turn, dc in 4th ch from hook and in next ch, dc in next dc (**beginning**

increase made)), dc in next 2 dc, dc in top of turning ch (turning ch counts as dc now and throughout), work **end Block increase** as follows: (YO, insert hook into base of last dc, pull up a loop, YO, draw through one loop on hook, (YO, draw through 2 loops on hook) twice) 3 times.
Row 3: Work beginning increase, dc in next 3 dc (**Block over Block made**), (ch 2, skip 2 dc, dc in next dc (**Space over Block made**)), work Block over Block, work end Block increase.
Row 4: Work beginning increase, work Block over Block, work Space over Block, (work 2 dc in next Space, dc in next dc (**Block over Space made**)), work Space over Block, work Block over Block, work end Block increase.
Rows 5-8: Follow Chart.
Row 9: (Ch 3, turn, dc in next 3 dc (**beginning Block over Block made**)), work Block over Block, (ch 2, dc in next dc (**Space over Space made**)), follow chart across.
Rows 10-12: Follow Chart.
Row 13: (Turn, slip st in first 4 dc, ch 3 (**beginning decrease made**)), work 2 Blocks, work 3 Spaces, work 3 Blocks, work 3 Spaces, work 2 Blocks, leave remaining 3 sts unworked.
First Side — Row 14: Work beginning decrease, work 5 Blocks.
Row 15: Work beginning decrease, work 3 Blocks; finish off.
Second Side — Row 14: With **right** side facing, join thread with slip st in 3rd dc from First Side, ch 3, work 5 Blocks.
Row 15: Work beginning decrease, work 3 Blocks; do **not** finish off.
EDGING: Ch 6, sc in top of last dc of next row, ch 4, sc in top of middle dc between Sides, ch 4, sc in top of last dc of next row, ch 6, sc in top of last dc of next row, ch 6, skip 4 dc, sc in next dc, ch 6, sc in top of last dc in row, ch 6, sc in top of last dc in next row) 3 times, ch 6, skip next row, sc in side of next row, ch 6, skip next row, sc in top of last dc of next row, ch 6, sc in top of last dc of next row, continue around in the same manner to beginning ch-6; join with a slip st to first ch, finish off.

LARGE HEART

Ch 6 **loosely**.
Row 1: Dc in 4th ch from hook and in remaining 2 chs (**bottom Block made**).
Row 2 (Right side): (Ch 5, turn, dc in 4th ch from hook and in next ch, dc in next dc (**beginning increase made**)), dc in next 2 dc, dc in top of turning ch (turning ch counts as dc now and throughout), work **end Block increase** as follows: (YO, insert hook into base of last dc, pull up a loop, YO, draw through one loop on hook, (YO, draw through 2 loops on hook) twice) 3 times.
Row 3: Work beginning increase, dc in next 3 dc (**Block over Block made**), (ch 2, skip 2 dc, dc in next dc (**Space over Block made**)), work Block over Block, work end Block increase.
Row 4: Work beginning increase, work Block over Block, work Space over Block, (work 2 dc in next Space, dc in next dc (**Block over Space made**)), work Space over Block, work Block over Block, work end Block increase.
Rows 5-8: Follow Chart.
Row 9: Work beginning increase, work Block over Block, work Space over Block, work Block over Block, work Space over Block, work Block over Block, work Block over Space, work Space over Block, (ch 2, dc in next dc (**Space over Space**

made)), follow chart across.
Row 10: Follow Chart.
Rows 11-16: (Ch 3, turn, dc in next 3 dc (**beginning Block over Block made**)), follow chart across.
Row 17: (Turn, slip st in first 4 dc, ch 3 (**beginning decrease made**)), work 3 Blocks, work 4 Spaces, work 3 Blocks, work 4 Spaces, work 3 Blocks, leave remaining 3 sts unworked.
First Side — Row 18: Work beginning decrease, work 7 Blocks.
Row 19: Work beginning decrease, work 5 Blocks; finish off.
Second Side — Row 18: With **right** side facing, join thread with slip st in 3rd dc from First Side, ch 3, work 7 Blocks.
Row 19: Work beginning decrease, work 5 Blocks; do **not** finish off.
EDGING: Ch 6, sc in top of last dc of next row, ch 4, sc in top of middle dc between Sides, ch 4, sc in top of last dc of next row, ch 6, sc in top of last dc of next row, (ch 6, skip 4 dc, sc in top of next dc) 3 times, (ch 6, sc in top of last dc of next row) 3 times, ch 6, skip next row, sc in side of next row, ch 6, skip next row, sc in side of next row, ch 6, skip next row, sc in top of last dc in next row, ch 6, sc in top of last dc in next row, continue around in same manner to beginning ch-6; join with a slip st to first ch, finish off.

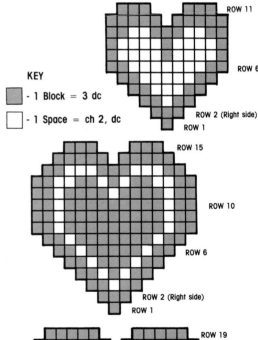

KEY
- 1 Block = 3 dc
- 1 Space = ch 2, dc

(Chart labels: ROW 11, ROW 6, ROW 2 (Right side), ROW 1)

(Chart labels: ROW 15, ROW 10, ROW 6, ROW 2 (Right side), ROW 1)

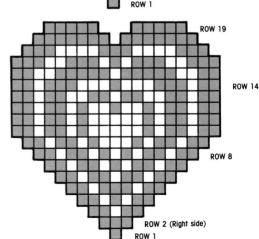

(Chart labels: ROW 19, ROW 14, ROW 8, ROW 2 (Right side), ROW 1)

SCHERENSCHNITTE DECORATIONS (Shown on page 52.)

You will need parchment paper; small, sharp-pointed scissors; large, sharp needle; instant coffee; cotton swab; transparent tape; paper towels, and small terry towel.
For finishing projects, you will need mat board and frame for Angels, approx. 6¼" x 9" sheet of colored stationery with matching envelope for Wreath, ecru thread for Tree, and rubber cement or craft glue.

CUTTING PAPER
1. Place parchment paper over desired design. (**Note:** Be sure to use paper large enough to accommodate entire design.) Trace design and fold line (indicated by dashes) onto paper. The traced side will be the back of finished project.
2. Fold parchment paper along fold line. To prevent movement of paper while cutting, tape the open edges of paper closed.
3. When cutting paper, always begin in the center of the design and work toward outer edge. This gives a larger area to hold while cutting and prevents paper from becoming limp. To cut out an area, pierce paper in center of area with point of scissors, then carefully cut along traced line. Cut small areas first, larger areas next, and outer edge last. For smoother cutting, keep scissors still and feed paper into scissors.
4. For small holes in Angels and Tree designs, lay paper on folded terry towel. Use needle to pierce holes where indicated by dots on designs.
5. After cutting, unfold paper and press with a warm iron to remove fold line (do not press Tree design).

AGING PAPER
1. If an antiqued look is desired (as shown on the Angels and Wreath designs), add 3 teaspoons instant coffee to ½ cup boiling water. Allow to cool.
2. Lay paper on paper towels and use one end of a cotton swab to apply coffee to the edges of the paper only. Dip other end of swab in water and blend coffee toward center of design. Repeat aging technique until paper is desired shade. (**Note:** If paper curls after it has dried, press with a warm iron.)

FINISHING PROJECTS
1. For Angels design, glue design on a piece of mat board and frame as desired. (Our design was custom framed.)
2. For Wreath design, match short edges and fold stationery in half. Center and glue design on front.
3. For Tree design, cut out two trees and erase pencil marks. Place trees together, matching fold lines. Machine or hand stitch (use a double strand of thread when hand stitching) along fold, leaving 8" of thread at top of trees for hanger. Knot ends of thread together and trim ends. Fold trees outward from seam to form a three-dimensional ornament.

ANGELS

WREATH

TREE

VICTORIAN STOCKING (Shown on page 50.)

BATTENBURG LACE TRIM

You will need 1½ yds of 8mm ecru lace tape (available at needlework shops that specialize in smocking and French hand sewing), ecru sewing thread, contrasting sewing thread for basting, #30 or #40 cotton crochet thread, #8 embroidery needle, #24 tapestry needle, 8" x 10" piece of clear plastic (the plastic from a zip-lock type food storage bag works well for this), 8" x 10" piece of non-fusible interfacing, and permanent felt-tip pen.

Note: While making Battenburg lace, always remember that the **wrong side** of your work is facing you.

1. Place plastic over pattern. Using permanent pen, trace around grey areas of pattern on page 58.
2. Place ink side of plastic on interfacing; baste together.
3. Cut tape into the following lengths: 13", 19", and 21".
4. For upper band of lace, use 19" length of lace tape. Beginning at **X** at upper left corner and leaving ½" extending (to fold and tack later), pin the lace tape to the pattern. To fold first corner, follow **Fig. 1a** to fold free end of lace tape away from pattern; press with finger. Following **Fig. 1b**, fold lace tape a second time toward pattern (folded edge will be even with edge of lace tape); pin. Fold the next two corners in the same manner. For last corner (at **X** on pattern), trim end to ½" if necessary. Fold each end of lace tape ¼" to wrong side; press with finger. Fold each end of lace tape again ¼" to wrong side; pin. (**Note:** Folded ends will lie on top of each other.)

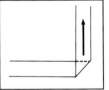

Fig. 1a   **Fig. 1b**

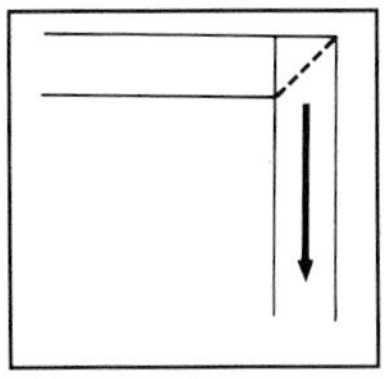

5. For first lace points, use 21" length of lace tape. Beginning at ● at left edge and leaving ½" extending, pin the lace tape to the pattern. To fold points, follow **Fig. 2a** to fold free end of lace tape away from pattern; press with finger. Follow **Fig. 2b** to fold lace tape a second time toward pattern (folded edge will be even with edge of lace tape); pin. Trim end of lace tape at ● at right edge to ½" if necessary. Fold ends of lace tape at ●'s ¼" to wrong side; press with finger. Fold ends of lace tape again ¼" to wrong side; pin. Repeat process for remaining points using the 13" length of lace tape, beginning and ending at ▲'s.

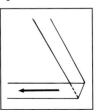 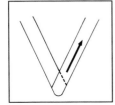

Fig. 2a   **Fig. 2b**

6. Using contrasting sewing thread and embroidery needle, baste tape to pattern. Remove pins.
7. Using single strand of ecru sewing thread and embroidery needle, begin at an intersection and tack the lace tape together wherever it touches or overlaps. To move from section to section, whipstitch along the edge of the lace tape. To end stitching, knot thread at an intersection.
8. Using crochet thread and tapestry needle, work the Double Russian Stitch (**Figs. 3a, 3b,** and **3c**) to fill in the upper band of the lace. (**Note:** Tension should be loose when working all filling stitches; do not pull stitches too tightly.)

DOUBLE RUSSIAN STITCH: For foundation bar, follow **Fig. 3a** and go down at 1; come up at 2. Whipstitch along inside left edge of tape and come up at 3. Bring needle under bar, keeping thread below point of needle as shown in **Fig. 3a**; pull needle through. Following **Fig. 3b** and keeping thread below point of needle, come up at inside edge of the lace tape approx. ¼" away from the first stitch; pull needle through. Continue working in this manner, spacing stitches approx. ¼" apart, until row is completed.
Turn work upside down. Whipstitch along inside left edge of tape and come up at 1 (**Fig. 3c**). Bring needle under bar, keeping thread below point of needle as shown in **Fig. 3c**; pull needle through. Following **Fig. 3b** and keeping thread below point of needle, come up at inside edge of the lace tape approx. ¼" away from the first stitch; pull needle through. Continue working in this manner, placing stitches between those on foundation bar and spacing stitches approx. ¼" apart, until row is completed.

Fig. 3a

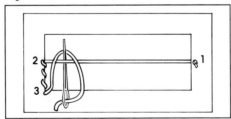

Fig. 3b

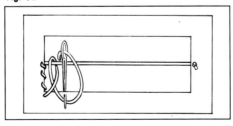

Fig. 3c

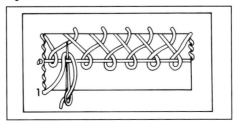

9. Use the English Wheel Stitch (**Figs. 4a, 4b,** and **4c**) to fill in the inner points of the lace. Use the Connected English Wheel Stitch (**Fig. 5**, page 58), a variation of the English Wheel, to fill in the rectangular shaped sections at each side of the lace.

ENGLISH WHEEL STITCH: For wheel spokes, follow **Fig. 4a** and go down at 1; come up at 2. Whipstitch along inside edge of tape; then go down at 3 and come up at 4. Whipstitch along inside edge of tape and go down at 5. Beginning with Spoke 1 as shown in **Fig. 4a**, bring needle under and over spokes. Work around three times. Following **Fig. 4b**, insert needle through wheel to lock stitch; come up at 6 and secure thread. (**Note:** Because the center point is larger, it has eight spokes. Follow **Fig. 4c** for placement of spokes on center point. Go down at odd numbers and come up at even numbers (1 — 7), whipstitching along inside edge of tape as necessary. Following **Fig. 4a** and beginning with Spoke 5, bring needle under and over spokes. Work around three times. Insert needle through wheel (**Fig. 4b**) to lock stitch. Come up at 8 and secure thread.

Fig. 4a

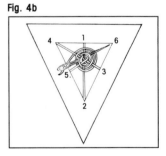

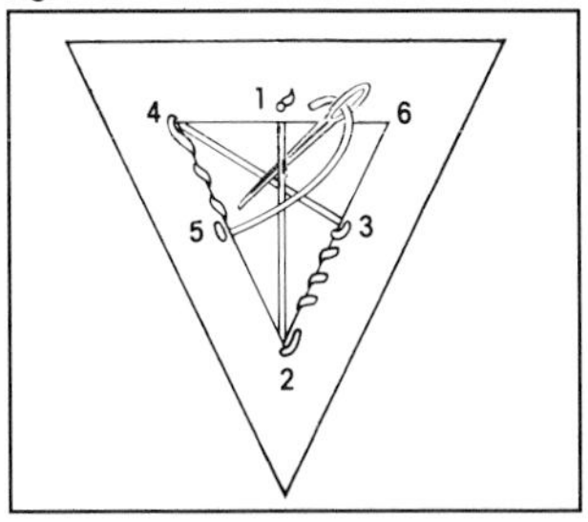

Fig. 4b

Fig. 4c

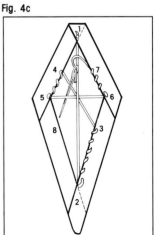

Continued on page 58.

VICTORIAN STOCKING (continued)

CONNECTED ENGLISH WHEEL STITCH: For wheel spokes, follow **Fig. 5** and go down at **1**, come up at **2**; go down at **3**, come up at **4**. Whipstitch along inside edge of tape and go down at **5**. Going down at odd numbers and up at even numbers, continue with stitches **6 — 15**. Whipstitch between stitches as necessary. For first wheel, beginning with Spoke 3, bring needle under and over spokes. Work around three times. Following **Fig. 4b** of the English Wheel Stitch, insert needle through wheel to lock stitch. Beginning with Spoke 7 (**Fig. 5**), work second wheel. Beginning with Spoke 1, work third wheel; then come up at **16** and secure thread.

Fig. 5

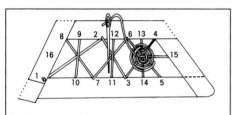

10. Clip basting threads. Remove lace from the pattern. To block lace, mist with water and press with iron until dry.

STOCKING

You will need completed Battenburg Lace Trim, ¼ yd of ecru linen, ½ yd of green velvet, ½ yd of ecru taffeta, tracing paper, thread to match fabrics, and 4" of ⅛"w green velvet ribbon for hanger.

1. For Stocking pattern (see Bear Stocking, pages 20 and 21), trace thick lines of entire Stocking pattern onto tracing paper, beginning with cuff and matching arrows and ▲'s; cut out. With velvet folded in half and cutting through both thicknesses, cut out front and back of Stocking. With taffeta folded in half and cutting through both thicknesses, cut out front and back of Stocking lining.
2. Trace Cuff pattern, on page 59, onto tracing paper; cut out. Fold linen in half and place pattern on fold as indicated; cut out Cuff. Repeat for second Cuff.
3. (**Note:** Unless otherwise indicated, use ¼" seam allowance throughout.) With right sides facing and leaving top edge open, sew front and back of Stocking together; repeat for lining. Clip curves. Turn Stocking (not lining) right side out.

4. With right sides facing, sew Cuff pieces together along sides and bottom edge. Clip corners and turn right side out; press. Beginning at the bottom left finished edge of Cuff, whipstitch or machine zigzag stitch Battenburg Lace Trim to bottom Cuff.
5. Refer to photo for position of front of Stocking (toe is facing right). Placing Cuff on Stocking and matching raw edges, sew pieces together using ½" seam allowance. Fold top edge of Stocking ½" to wrong side; press.
6. With wrong sides together, insert lining into Stocking. Fold top edge of lining ¾" to wrong side and pin to Stocking.
7. For hanger, fold velvet ribbon in half. Place ends between lining and Stocking at left seam line; pin in place with approx. 1½" extending above Stocking.
8. Slipstitch lining to Stocking and, at the same time, securely sew hanger in place.

BATTENBURG LACE PATTERN

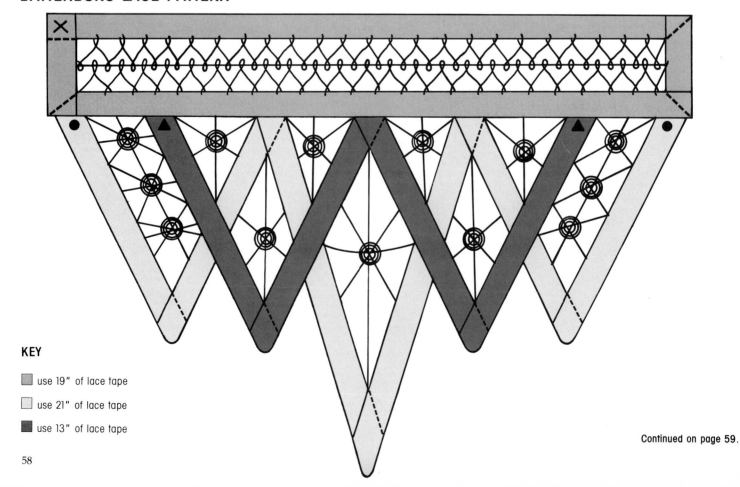

KEY

■ use 19" of lace tape

□ use 21" of lace tape

■ use 13" of lace tape

Continued on page 59.

VICTORIAN STOCKING
(continued)

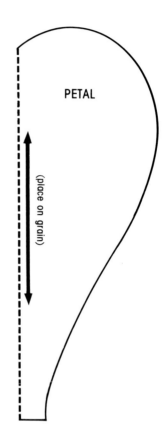

PETAL

(place on grain)

Place on fold

CUFF
(cut 2)

PAPER ROSES (Shown on page 50.)

For each rose, you will need off-white or desired color crepe paper (packaged in folded sheets), green florist wire, green florist tape, clusters of pepper berries, wire cutters, hot glue gun, and glue sticks.

1. Use petal pattern on this page and follow **Transferring Patterns**, page 157.
2. Remove crepe paper from package and keep folded. Matching arrow on pattern to grain of paper, draw around pattern on top layer of paper. Cut out petals, cutting through all thicknesses. (**Note:** You will need 13 petals for each rose and 5 petals for each rosebud.) Repeat for desired number of roses.
3. Place wire on lower section of first petal as shown in **Fig. 1**. Wrap petal around wire. Cover wrapped section of petal and approx. 5" of wire with florist tape.

Fig. 1

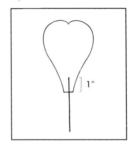

1"

4. Shape remaining petals by gently pulling outward at sides to create a cupped effect.
5. Overlapping each petal, place four petals around wire and wrap with florist tape as in Step 3. (**Note:** If making rosebud, continue with Step 6.) To complete rose, add two more rows of four petals each.
6. Cut wire to desired length and cover any unwrapped wire with florist tape.
7. Glue a cluster of pepper berries to center of rose.

PAPIER-MÂCHÉ BALLS

(Shown on page 50.)

For each ball, you will need newspaper, wheat paste or wallpaper paste, desired size Styrofoam® ball (we used 2" and 3" dia. balls), gesso, 1"w paintbrush, gold or desired color spray paint, a straight pin, craft glue, and nylon line for hanger.

1. Cut paper into approx. ⅜" x 6" strips.
2. Mix approx. ½ cup paste with water according to manufacturer's instructions.
3. Dip strips in paste and pull strips between two fingers to remove excess paste. Wrap strips around ball, smoothing wrinkles with fingers. Overlapping strips, continue wrapping until ball is covered; allow to dry.
4. Apply gesso to ball; allow to dry.
5. Spray paint ball; allow to dry. It may be necessary to use more than one coat to get even coverage.
6. For hanger, cut 8" of nylon line and knot ends of line together. Push pin through knot; dip pin in glue. Push pin into top of ball.

WREATH (Shown on page 51.)

You will need an artificial evergreen wreath (we used a 26" dia. wreath), desired number of paper roses and rosebuds (see Paper Roses, on this page), clusters of pepper berries, white baby's breath, 1¼"w gold metallic ribbon, green florist wire, hot glue gun, and glue sticks.

1. Referring to photo for placement, insert stems of roses into wreath and twist wire stems around wreath to secure.
2. Referring to photo, glue clusters of pepper berries and baby's breath to wreath.
3. Make a multi-loop bow with streamers using gold ribbon. Referring to photo, wire bow to wreath.

Among the pines and vines of the deep woods, away from the noise of the city, the spirit of Father Christmas can be felt. Just close your eyes and imagine his saintly figure traveling through the forests from town to town, spreading Christmas cheer and goodwill. Along the way, he might have watched with affection the flight of a bright cardinal, or stopped to pick up a fallen pinecone to admire its perfect form.

In this collection, we present a distinctive holiday look combining the gentle charm of Olde World Santas and the tranquility of decorations that spring from the earth. Images of Santa take many shapes for stencil painting and cross stitching. A painted grapevine garland trimmed with bright berries encircles the tree and spirals across the mantel. Baskets are brimming with a deep woods harvest of pinecones, lotus pods, and sweet gum balls. A flock of cardinals adds touches of vivid red, and delicate clusters of white statice soften the room with lacy foliage.

Instructions for creating this woodsy Olde World Christmas begin on page 68. This year, enjoy a quiet Christmas among the pines and vines.

Our **Olde Santas Wreath** *(page 70)* brings wishes for a Merry Olde Christmas. A grapevine wreath trimmed with eucalyptus and canella berries frames the four old-fashioned Santas, which are created with counted cross stitch.

Candles add a warm glow to the holiday season, and these **Painted Candles** *(page 69)* shine with Christmas cheer. The **Santa Shaped Candles** *(page 70)* are formed in candy molds.

An arrangement of fruit is always pretty, but these **Sumac Apples** *(page 70)* have everlasting beauty. Each is actually a Styrofoam® ball covered with sumac berries.

The peacefulness of the forest dwells in this lovely centerpiece, a grapevine tree decorated to match the large tree shown on page 60. Miniature cardinals have made their home in its array of Spanish moss, dried white German statice, pinecones, eucalyptus, and sumac.

This **Bird's Nest Potpourri** (*page 70*) has a woodsy scent that complements the pines and vines used in your Christmas decor. Tiny **Moss Wreaths** (*page 69*) like this one can be trimmed as you please for lots of different looks.

All the little redbirds on our tree are nesting on **Moss Wreaths** *(page 69)* atop clusters of dried white German statice. Each wreath is trimmed with a circle of eucalyptus and canella berries. The tree's colorful garland is made by spray painting grapevines glossy red and adding long-stemmed artificial red berries. When loose grapevines aren't available, unbind a few large grapevine wreaths and soak them in water four to six hours; untwist the vines and allow them to dry overnight before painting.

Relatives and friends on your Christmas list will love these handmade cards and gift tags created with **Olde Santa Stencils** *(page 68)*. A **Pine Needle Basket** *(page 70)* makes a pleasing place to put your holiday cards and keepsakes.

Invite the spirit of Christmas into your home with a portrait of Santa that reflects his loving generosity. Our **Father Christmas Banner** *(page 71)* captures this spirit in counted cross stitch.

Through the years, different cultures have dressed Santa in coats of many colors. This **Olde Santas Wall Hanging** *(page 70)* features four nostalgic images of Santa in counted cross stitch. Our color charts make stitching the designs extra easy, and light brown linen gives the needlework an antique appearance.

Evergreen print paper gives your gifts a woodsy touch. To make this pretty paper, unroll some plain wrapping paper, scatter sprigs of arborvitae or other type of evergreen on it, and lightly spray it with paint. We tied our packages with deep red ribbon and trimmed them with eucalyptus and dried berries, stenciled gift tags, and fringed cross stitch ornaments.

We gathered these baskets of beautiful gifts from nature to place beneath our woodland tree. They're brimming with lotus pods, pinecones, and sweet gum balls, plus dried white German statice, sumac, eucalyptus, pine needles, and canella berries. A contented cardinal keeps watch over our treasures.

OLDE SANTA STENCILS (Shown on page 65.)

For each Santa design, you will need three pieces of Mylar® or sheets of clear, flexible plastic (3"w x 4"h for small Santa and 3½"w x 5"h for large Santa); red, flesh, white, green, and black acrylic paint; five small stencil brushes; craft knife; black permanent felt-tip pen with fine point; removable tape (this special tape is easy to remove from paper and is available at hobby or art supply stores); paper towels; transparent tape (for repairing stencils, if needed), and a thick layer of newspapers or a cutting mat.

For large Santa card, you will also need desired number of 6¼" x 9" lightweight sheets of ivory stationery with matching envelopes (match short edges and fold stationery in half), and a black felt-tip calligraphy pen with fine point.

For small Santa gift tag, you will also need desired number of 3¼" x 3¾" pieces of parchment paper (match short edges and fold paper in half).

CUTTING STENCILS
1. For each design, you will need to cut three stencils. For first stencil, center one piece of Mylar® over pattern #1 of desired size Santa. Use permanent pen to trace solid and dashed lines onto Mylar®. (The dashed lines will be used for placement.) Write the number "1" in one corner of stencil.

2. Repeat Step 1 to trace patterns #2 and #3. Write the number of each pattern in one corner of the stencil.

3. To cut each stencil, place Mylar® on a surface covered with a thick layer of newspapers or on a cutting mat. Use craft knife to carefully cut along **solid lines** of design. (**Note:** If you accidentally cut or tear stencil, tape both sides of tear with transparent tape; recut shape.)

PAINTING DESIGNS
1. Position #1 stencil on paper; tape in place with removable tape. (**Note:** For card, position stencil to allow space for "Merry Olde Santa" phrase.)

2. Always use a clean, dry stencil brush for each color of paint. Dip brush into paint and remove excess paint by stroking brush on paper towels. Brush should be almost dry to produce a good stencil. Using red paint and beginning at edge of cutout area, apply paint with an up-and-down stamping motion. Working from edge of design to center, keep paint darker at the edge than at center. Allow paint to dry and remove stencil.

3. Position #2 stencil on paper, using dashed lines for placement; tape in place with removable tape. Follow Step 2 to paint boots and mittens black, tree green, and face flesh. Allow paint to dry and remove stencil.

4. Position #3 stencil on paper, using dashed lines for placement; tape in place with removable tape. Follow Step 2 to paint beard white. Allow paint to dry and remove stencil.

5. Wash brushes and stencils in warm, soapy water and rinse thoroughly.

6. For phrase on card, place unfolded card over pattern. Use calligraphy pen to trace words onto card.

PAINTED CANDLES (Shown on page 63.)

You will need desired size taper or pillar candles, desired colors of acrylic paint, small round paintbrush, tracing paper, transparent tape, and sharp pointed needle.

1. For tapers, trace desired patterns on this page onto tracing paper. (**Note:** Patterns can only be used one time.)
2. For pillar candles, trace desired size Santa pattern on this page onto tracing paper.
3. Referring to photo for placement, position patterns on candles and tape in place. To transfer design to candle, use needle to ``draw'' over pattern. Remove any remaining paper from candles.
4. Referring to photo, paint candles. Allow to dry.

MOSS WREATHS (Shown on pages 64 and 65.)

For each wreath, you will need one 4" x 4" piece of medium-weight cardboard, tracing paper, utility or craft knife, Spanish moss, thread to match moss, eucalyptus, clusters of canella berries, desired color ⅛"w ribbon (optional), hot glue gun, and glue sticks.

1. Trace wreath pattern onto tracing paper and cut out.
2. Draw around pattern on cardboard. Use utility or craft knife to cut out wreath.

3. Place Spanish moss on one side of cardboard. To secure moss, wrap thread around moss and cardboard.
4. Referring to diagrams, glue eucalyptus and clusters of canella berries to top center of wreath or around entire wreath. If desired, glue a multi-loop bow to top center of wreath.

DIAGRAMS

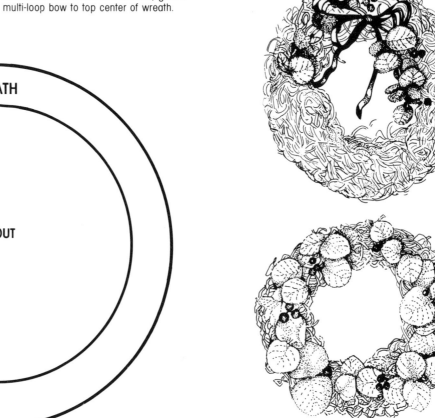

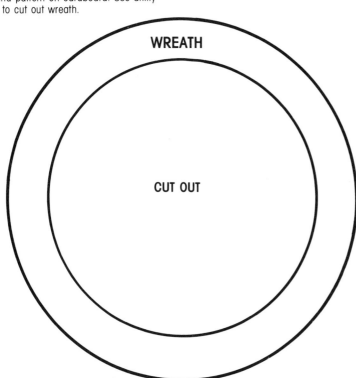

WREATH

CUT OUT

SUMAC APPLES

(Shown on page 63.)

For each apple, you will need one Styrofoam® ball (we used a 4" dia. ball), red spray paint, sumac berries, one twig, artificial leaves, and craft glue.

1. To make an apple that will sit on a tabletop, flatten one side of ball by pressing it against a flat surface.
2. Spray paint ball; allow to dry.
3. Working on one section of ball at a time, cover ball with glue and press sumac berries firmly into glue; allow to dry thoroughly. If necessary, glue more berries on ball to fill in any spaces.
4. Referring to photo, insert twig into top of ball for stem; glue leaves to twig.

BIRD'S NEST POTPOURRI

(Shown on page 64.)

For potpourri, you will need ¼ cup canella berries, ½ cup hazelnuts and almonds (in shells), I cup fresh pine needles, 1 cup sweet gum balls, 1 cup eucalyptus cut in 3" pieces, 20 drops woodsy musk oil, and glass jar with tight-fitting lid.

For nest, you will need a small round basket or purchased nest (we used a 6" dia. basket), one small artificial cardinal, and small piece of plastic wrap to line basket.

1. Mix ingredients for potpourri and place in jar. Secure lid on jar. Place jar in a cool, dark, dry place for two weeks. Every few days, shake jar to mix contents.
2. Line basket or nest with plastic wrap to prevent oil from seeping through and damaging any surfaces. Place potpourri in basket and set bird on edge of basket.

SANTA SHAPED CANDLES

(Shown on page 63.)

For each candle, you will need paraffin, 2-piece Santa candy mold (we used a 4½" mold), vegetable oil, pencil, candlewick, double boiler or electric frying pan, large can for melting wax in frying pan, newspapers, craft knife, transparent tape, desired colors of acrylic paint, and small paintbrush.

1. **Caution: Do not melt paraffin over an open flame or directly on burner.** Cover work area with newspapers. Melt paraffin over hot water in double boiler or in a large can placed in an electric frying pan filled with water.
2. Lightly oil mold. Cut wick the length of the mold plus 3". Place wick inside mold with approx. ½" extending at top center of mold. Turn mold upside down and prop mold so it will remain straight. Wind wick at bottom of mold around pencil, and tape in place. Lay pencil across bottom of mold, keeping wick centered.
3. Pour wax into mold. Allow wax to harden. Remove Santa from mold and trim any uneven edges with craft knife. Trim wick at base of candle.
4. Referring to photo, paint candle.

PINE NEEDLE BASKET

(Shown on page 65.)

You will need a small rectangular basket with a flat bottom and straight sides (we used a 5"w x 3½"d x 4"h basket), pine needles approx. 1" longer than height of basket, small pinecones, cluster of canella berries, eucalyptus, hot glue gun, and glue sticks.

1. Place basket on its side. Place a line of hot glue approx. 1½" from bottom of basket. Press a small cluster of pine needles into glue (**Fig. 1**). Some glue may come between needles, but it will be covered later. Cover all sides of basket with needles.

Fig. 1

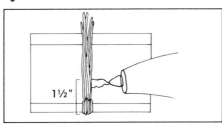

2. Trim needles to 1" above top of basket rim.
3. Referring to photo, glue a row of eucalyptus on needles to cover glue line.
4. Referring to photo for placement, glue an arrangement of eucalyptus, pinecones, and berries to one long side of basket.

OLDE SANTAS WREATH

(Shown on page 62.)

You will need eight 5" x 7" pieces of Light Brown Linen (26 ct), embroidery floss (see color keys, pages 72 and 73), embroidery hoop (optional), polyester fiberfill, one grapevine wreath (we used a 14" dia. wreath), eucalyptus, clusters of canella berries, parchment paper, black felt-tip pen, hot glue gun, and glue sticks.

1. Following **Working on Linen**, page 157, center each Olde Santa design (pages 72 and 73) on one piece of fabric. (**Note:** Four remaining pieces of fabric will be used as backing fabric.) Work each design over two fabric threads, using 2 strands of floss for Cross Stitch, 1 for Backstitch, and 1 for French Knots.
2. For each shaped ornament, place right sides of stitched piece and backing fabric together. Leaving an opening for turning and stuffing, sew fabric pieces together ¼" from edges of design. Leaving a ¼" seam allowance, cut out design. Clip curves and turn right side out. Lightly stuff ornament with fiberfill and sew final closure by hand.
3. To decorate wreath, refer to photo and glue eucalyptus and clusters of canella berries to wreath.
4. Cut parchment paper 1¾"w and desired length to lay across top of wreath. Using felt-tip pen, center and write "Merry Olde Christmas" on paper; crumple paper and press flat again with fingers. Referring to photo for placement, lay paper across top of wreath and trim ends as desired; glue paper to wreath.
5. Referring to photo for placement, glue ornaments to wreath.

OLDE SANTAS WALL HANGING

(Shown on page 66.)

You will need eight 5" x 7" pieces of Light Brown Linen (26 ct), embroidery floss (see color keys, pages 72 and 73), embroidery hoop (optional), polyester fiberfill, 1½ yds of 1½"w grosgrain ribbon, thread to match ribbon, and one small plastic ring for hanger.

1. Following **Working on Linen**, page 157, center each Olde Santa design (pages 72 and 73) on one piece of fabric. (**Note:** Four remaining pieces of fabric will be used as backing fabric.) Work each design over two fabric threads, using 2 strands of floss for Cross Stitch, 1 for Backstitch, and 1 for French Knots.
2. For each fringed ornament, place wrong sides of stitched piece and backing fabric together. Use desired color of floss to cross stitch fabric pieces together ½" from design along sides and bottom edge. Lightly stuff with fiberfill. Cross stitch across top of ornament ½" from design. Trim fabric to ½" from cross stitched lines; fringe fabric to stitched lines.
3. For wall hanging, cut ribbon into 36", 14½", and 3½" lengths. Using 36" length of ribbon, fold one end under 1½"; tack in place.
4. For bow, use 14½" length of ribbon and overlap ends ½" to form a loop (**Fig. 1**); tack in place. Wrap 3½" length of ribbon around center of loop and overlap ends ½" in back; tack in place (**Fig. 2**). Center and tack bow ¾" from folded edge of ribbon.

Fig. 1

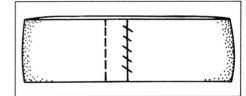

Fig. 2

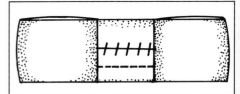

5. Referring to photo, tack one ornament to ribbon 1¼" below bow. Tack remaining ornaments to ribbon 1¼" apart.
6. Referring to photo, notch bottom edge of ribbon.
7. For hanger, tack plastic ring to back of bow.

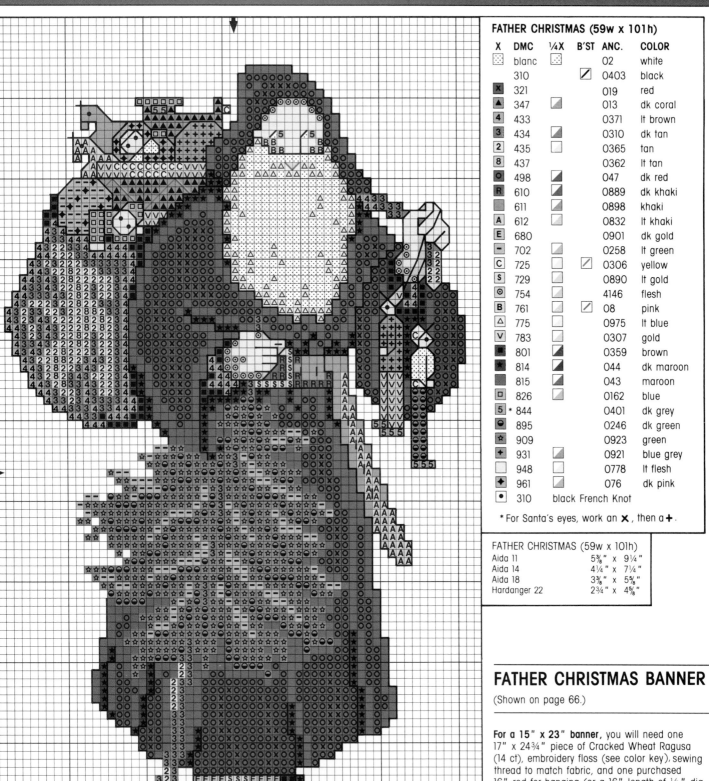

FATHER CHRISTMAS (59w x 101h)

X	DMC	¼X	B'ST	ANC.	COLOR
⠂	blanc	⠂		02	white
	310		╱	0403	black
X	321			019	red
▲	347	◣		013	dk coral
4	433			0371	lt brown
3	434	◣		0310	dk tan
2	435	◹		0365	tan
8	437			0362	lt tan
◉	498	◣		047	dk red
R	610	◣		0889	dk khaki
	611	◣		0898	khaki
A	612	◹		0832	lt khaki
E	680	◣		0901	dk gold
–	702	◣		0258	lt green
C	725	◹	╱	0306	yellow
S	729	◹		0890	lt gold
◉	754	◹		4146	flesh
B	761		╱	08	pink
△	775	◹		0975	lt blue
V	783	◹		0307	gold
■	801	◣		0359	brown
★	814	◣		044	dk maroon
	815	◣		043	maroon
▢	826	◹		0162	blue
5	* 844			0401	dk grey
◒	895			0246	dk green
☆	909			0923	green
✚	931	◣		0921	blue grey
	948	◹		0778	lt flesh
✦	961	◣		076	dk pink
•	310			black French Knot

*For Santa's eyes, work an **X**, then a **+**.

FATHER CHRISTMAS (59w x 101h)	
Aida 11	5⅜" x 9¼"
Aida 14	4¼" x 7¼"
Aida 18	3⅜" x 5⅝"
Hardanger 22	2¾" x 4⅝"

FATHER CHRISTMAS BANNER

(Shown on page 66.)

For a 15" x 23" banner, you will need one 17" x 24¾" piece of Cracked Wheat Ragusa (14 ct), embroidery floss (see color key), sewing thread to match fabric, and one purchased 16" rod for hanging (or a 16" length of ½" dia. dowel and two end caps stained desired color).

1. Center design on fabric. Work design over two fabric threads, using 6 strands of floss for Cross Stitch, 2 for Backstitch, and 2 for French Knots.
2. For wall hanging, fold side edges under ½" and press; fold under ½" again and hem. For casing, fold top edge under ¼" and press; fold under 1½" and hem. For fringe, machine stitch 1¾" from bottom edge and unravel fabric to stitched line.
3. Insert rod through casing and attach end caps.

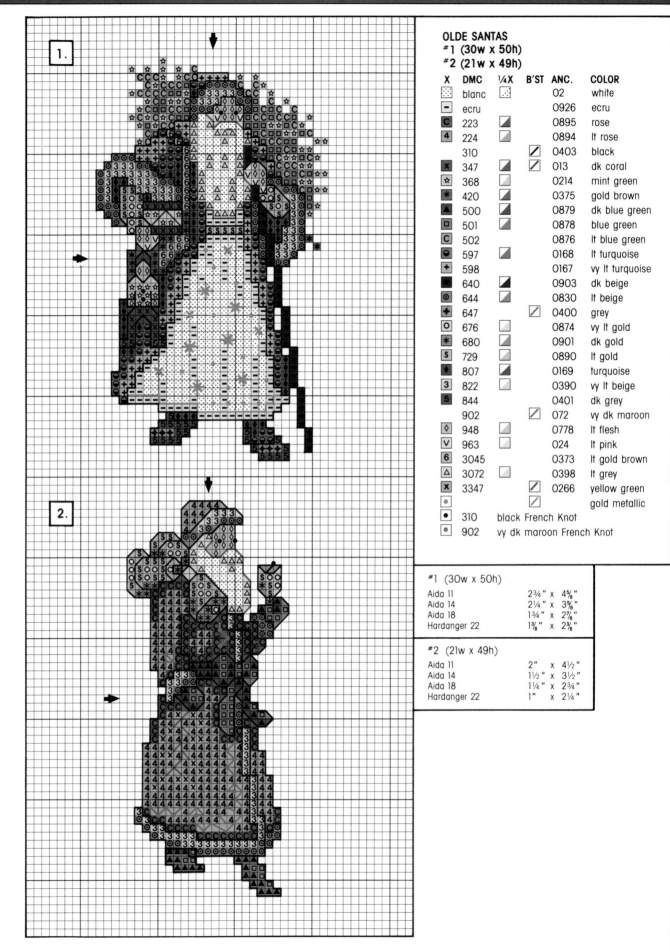

1.

2.

OLDE SANTAS
#1 (30w x 50h)
#2 (21w x 49h)

X	DMC	¼X	B'ST	ANC.	COLOR
▫	blanc	▫		02	white
−	ecru			0926	ecru
C	223	◩		0895	rose
4	224	◩		0894	lt rose
	310		◪	0403	black
X	347	◩	◪	013	dk coral
☆	368	◩		0214	mint green
✳	420	◩		0375	gold brown
▲	500	◩		0879	dk blue green
▢	501	◩		0878	blue green
C	502			0876	lt blue green
◉	597	◩		0168	lt turquoise
✚	598			0167	vy lt turquoise
▓	640	◩		0903	dk beige
◉	644	◩		0830	lt beige
✦	647		◪	0400	grey
O	676			0874	vy lt gold
✳	680	◩		0901	dk gold
S	729	◩		0890	lt gold
◆	807	◩		0169	turquoise
3	822	◩		0390	vy lt beige
5	844			0401	dk grey
	902		◪	072	vy dk maroon
◇	948	◩		0778	lt flesh
V	963	◩		024	lt pink
6	3045			0373	lt gold brown
△	3072	◩		0398	lt grey
X	3347	◩	◪	0266	yellow green
•			◪		gold metallic
●	310		black French Knot		
⦿	902		vy dk maroon French Knot		

#1 (30w x 50h)		
Aida 11	2¾" x	4⅝"
Aida 14	2¼" x	3⅝"
Aida 18	1¾" x	2⅞"
Hardanger 22	1⅜" x	2⅜"

#2 (21w x 49h)		
Aida 11	2" x	4½"
Aida 14	1½" x	3½"
Aida 18	1¼" x	2¾"
Hardanger 22	1" x	2¼"

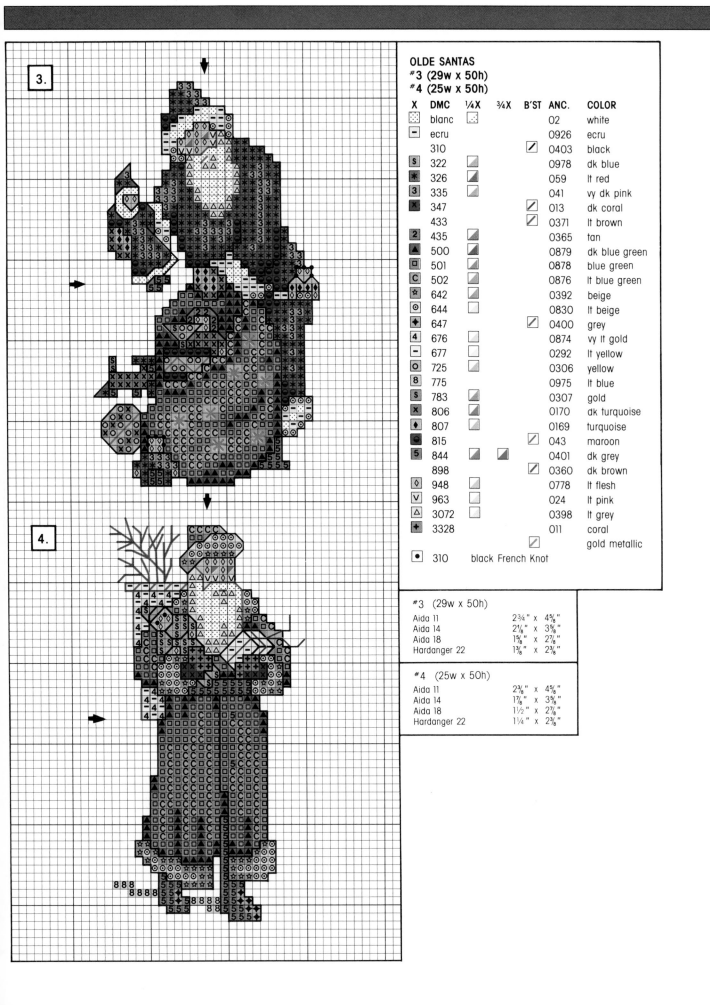

OLDE SANTAS
#3 (29w x 50h)
#4 (25w x 50h)

X	DMC	¼X	¾X	B'ST	ANC.	COLOR
⣿	blanc	⣿			02	white
−	ecru				0926	ecru
	310			◸	0403	black
S	322	◨			0978	dk blue
✳	326	◨			059	lt red
3	335	◨			041	vy dk pink
✕	347			◸	013	dk coral
	433			◸	0371	lt brown
2	435	◨			0365	tan
▲	500	◨			0879	dk blue green
▣	501	◨			0878	blue green
C	502	◨			0876	lt blue green
✩	642	◨			0392	beige
⊙	644	◻			0830	lt beige
✦	647			◸	0400	grey
4	676	◻			0874	vy lt gold
−	677	◻			0292	lt yellow
o	725	◻			0306	yellow
8	775				0975	lt blue
S	783	◨			0307	gold
✕	806	◨			0170	dk turquoise
◆	807	◨			0169	turquoise
⬢	815			◸	043	maroon
5	844	◨	◨		0401	dk grey
	898			◸	0360	dk brown
◇	948	◨			0778	lt flesh
V	963	◻			024	lt pink
△	3072	◻			0398	lt grey
✚	3328				011	coral
				◸		gold metallic
●	310		black French Knot			

#3 (29w x 50h)

Aida 11		2¾"	x 4⅝"
Aida 14		2⅛"	x 3⅝"
Aida 18		1⅝"	x 2⅞"
Hardanger 22		1⅜"	x 2⅜"

#4 (25w x 50h)

Aida 11		2⅜"	x 4⅝"
Aida 14		1⅞"	x 3⅝"
Aida 18		1½"	x 2⅞"
Hardanger 22		1¼"	x 2⅜"

T he magic of a white
Christmas lies not only in its
beauty but also in the gentle
mood it settles upon the earth.
A blanket of snow gives the
world a clean, fresh spirit and
slows the pace of life, allowing
us time to reflect on the
wonders of the season.

In this collection, we bring
you a sparkling array of
decorations that reflect the
beauty of winter's snow and
ice. The tree, rising above a
cloud of snowy white tulle, is
abloom with silk poinsettias in
silver and white. Fresh roses
add a pretty touch of pink. To
catch the light, silver balls
and glistening garlands are
hung all around, and up and
down. Elsewhere in the room,
reindeer silhouettes prance
above a silvery centerpiece that
mirrors the glow of
candlelight. Shining fabric
trees create an enchanting
little forest. White linens for
the table are adorned with
Scandinavian designs of
reindeer, trees, and
snowflakes. Even the gifts
have a wintry sparkle.

Instructions for these
projects and more begin on
page 80. This year, create a
winter wonderland for
Christmas and enjoy a
sparkling holiday season!

Pink roses and miniature carnations bring lovely color to this **Floral Wreath** *(page 82)*, while striking silk poinsettias provide its Christmas spirit. The wreath looks especially pretty when centered between **Mantel Corsages** *(page 80)*, as shown on pages 74 and 75.

These **Fabric Trees** *(page 82)* remind us of how ice-covered evergreens shimmer in the sunlight on a frosty winter day. Designed in three sizes, the trees are made of cardboard shapes covered with silver lamé.

An assortment of silvery decorations trims our elegant tree. There are garlands of shiny beads and stars, silver glass ball ornaments, and silk poinsettias dressed up with silver spray paint. Pink roses and baby's breath, kept fresh in florist water picks, add delicate color. A garland of snowy white tulle enhances the look.

Our treetop arrangement of roses, baby's breath, and decorative white sticks reaches toward the heavens and captures its own moon and stars. A cloud of white tulle sets off the arrangement. Florist water picks keep the flowers fresh. The shiny gold moon is one of our **Metallic Cutouts** *(page 80)*, and the stars are on a purchased garland.

Our **Winter Scent** *(page 82)* is a fragrant potpourri of pinecones, lotus pods, and evergreen sprigs. For sparkle, we set it on a mirror tile and added a metallic star cutout and garland.

Our **Reindeer Centerpiece** *(page 81)* makes it easy to imagine how the deer might frolic on a moonlit night in the winter woods. Silver spray paint on a thorn wreath and silk poinsettias reflects the warm glow of the candlelight, while metallic reindeer cutouts strike a graceful pose. Garlands of shiny beads and a mirror base add sparkle.

Our starry **Reindeer Wreath** (*page 81*) has a mirror in the center to reflect your holiday mood. Its moon, stars, and reindeer are easy-to-make **Metallic Cutouts** (*page 80*) crafted of lightweight mat board.

A dramatic arrangement of candles is an easy way to create an aura of elegance. And there's nothing to make! Just assemble some of your favorite pieces of silver and stemware — old or new, matching or not. Our arrangement includes rose-shaped floating candles in crystal sherbet glasses filled with water, tapers in silver candlesticks, and votives in small glass candle holders. Fresh flowers provide the finishing touch.

These elegant gift wraps begin with glistening white and silver wrapping papers. Their trimmings include white and silver ribbons, shiny garlands, metallic cutouts, glass ball ornaments, and silk poinsettias.

Your holiday table will receive rave reviews when you set it with these elegant **Christmas Table Linens** *(page 84)*. Their Scandinavian designs are cross stitched in frosty grey on white linen napkins, mini bags, personalized place cards, and a table runner.

Shining glass ball ornaments, partially filled with water, keep your holiday flowers fresh. These **Ornament Flower Vases** *(page 82)* can be propped upright for a pretty accent, or you can hang them on your tree.

To hold your holiday cards, dress up a painted basket. Ours is wrapped with a band of silver ribbon and trimmed with a white silk poinsettia and fresh evergreen sprigs.

MANTEL CORSAGES (Shown on pages 74 and 75.)

You will need two rectangular green plastic containers (we used two 5" x 10" containers), two blocks of water-absorbent floral foam (cut to fit containers), six bridal bouquet holders with floral foam cages, sharp knife, ¼"w waterproof florist tape, green florist wire, wire cutters, Springeraii fern, cedar greenery, approx. 30 fresh roses, and fresh baby's breath.

1. Immerse floral foam and bouquet holders in water for 15 minutes. Place blocks of floral foam in containers. If necessary, trim foam even with top edge of containers by cutting away excess with a knife. To secure foam in containers, place strips of waterproof tape across top of foam (Fig. 1).

Fig. 1

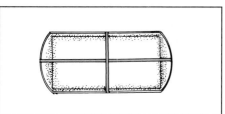

2. Following Fig. 2, tape three bouquet holders together underneath cages. Following Fig. 3, bring tape under top bouquet holder. Wrap tape around container twice to secure. Repeat for remaining bouquet holders and second container.

Fig. 2   Fig. 3

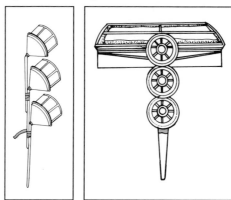

3. Referring to Fig. 4, insert wire into top of each rose stem just below the flower; wrap wire around stem. Place in water and set aside.

Fig. 4

4. Referring to photo for arrangement, insert fern and cedar firmly into floral foam in containers and bouquet holders. Referring to photo and trimming stems as necessary, insert roses and baby's breath into arrangement of greenery. If necessary, add additional fern to arrangement to fill in spaces.

METALLIC CUTOUTS (Shown on page 78.)

For each cutout, you will need silver or gold lightweight mat board (available at art supply stores), tracing paper, craft glue, sewing needle, and nylon line for hanger.

1. Trace desired pattern from this page or page 81 onto tracing paper and cut out.
2. (Note: Cutting on right side of metallic mat board produces a more finished look.) Place pattern on right side of mat board and draw around pattern. For reversed shape, turn pattern over and draw around it again. Cut out shapes.

3. With wrong sides facing, glue shapes together.
4. For hanger, use needle to make a small hole in top center of cutout; thread 8" of nylon line through hole and knot ends of line together.

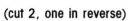

LARGE STAR

MEDIUM STAR

SMALL STAR

MOON

(cut 2, one in reverse)

(cut 2, one in reverse)

Continued on page 81.

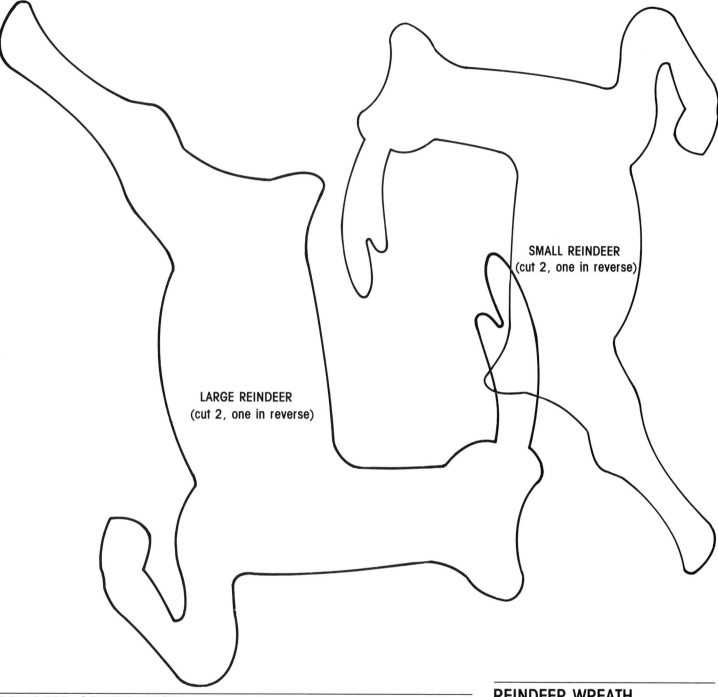

LARGE REINDEER
(cut 2, one in reverse)

SMALL REINDEER
(cut 2, one in reverse)

REINDEER CENTERPIECE (Shown on page 77.)

You will need one grapevine or thorn wreath (we used a 16" dia. thorn wreath); one 12" square mirror tile; one each of the following white pillar candles: 4"h, 6"h, and 9"h; 4 silk poinsettias; 2 silver large reindeer cutouts (see Metallic Cutouts, page 80; follow Steps 1 and 2 only); one 8" and one 9½" length of ¼" dia. dowel; silver and iridescent bead garlands; silver spray paint; wire cutters; hot glue gun, and glue sticks.

1. Spray paint wreath, poinsettias, and dowels; allow to dry. It may be necessary to use more than one coat to get an even coverage.

2. Referring to photo for placement, glue approx. 1" of one dowel to wrong side of one reindeer shape. With wrong sides facing, glue two reindeer shapes together. Repeat for remaining dowel and reindeer shapes.
3. Referring to photo for placement, insert 1" of each dowel into wreath; glue in place.
4. Trim stems of poinsettias to 1". Referring to photo for placement, glue poinsettias to wreath. Drape garlands on wreath; glue as necessary to secure.
5. Center wreath over mirror. Arrange candles in center of wreath. (**Note:** Do not leave wreath unattended while candles are burning.)

REINDEER WREATH

(Shown on page 78.)

You will need an artificial evergreen wreath (we used a 26" dia. wreath); round mirror approx. 3" larger than inside dia. of wreath; one silver large reindeer cutout, one gold moon cutout, and desired number of silver medium star cutouts (see Metallic Cutouts, page 80; omit hangers); silver star garland; hot glue gun, and glue sticks.

1. Hot glue mirror to back of wreath.
2. Referring to photo, place garland on wreath; glue as necessary to secure.
3. Referring to photo, position cutouts on wreath; glue in place.

ORNAMENT FLOWER VASES

(Shown on page 79.)

For each vase, you will need one silver glass ball ornament, one fresh rose, one fresh sprig of baby's breath, hot glue gun, glue sticks, and nylon line for hanger (optional).

1. Carefully remove cap from top of ornament. Place a small amount of hot glue on neck of ornament and carefully replace cap. (**Note:** To make a vase that will sit on a tabletop, apply a circle of hot glue to bottom of ornament. Allow to set.)
2. Fill ornament approx. half full with water (too much water will make the ornament too heavy to hang). Cut flower stems desired lengths. Insert stems through opening in top of cap.
3. If hanger is desired, thread 8" (or desired length) of nylon line through metal ring in cap; knot ends of line together.

WINTER SCENT (Shown on page 77.)

You will need one 8" dia. glass bowl, one 11" square mirror tile (we used one with a beveled edge), 22" of silver star garland, pinecones, lotus pods, purchased small white painted pinecones, fresh evergreen sprigs, one silver medium star cutout (see Metallic Cutouts, page 80; omit hanger), desired scent of essential oil, and a large container with tight-fitting lid.

1. Place pinecones, lotus pods, and evergreen sprigs in large container. Add 1 - 2 drops of essential oil. Secure lid on container. Place container in cool, dark, dry place for two weeks. Every few days, shake container to mix contents.
2. Place potpourri in glass bowl. Place star cutout in potpourri. Place bowl on mirror tile. Refer to photo and arrange garland, one pinecone, and one sprig of evergreen around outside of bowl.

FLORAL WREATH

(Shown on page 76.)

You will need an artificial evergreen wreath with pinecones (we used a 34" dia. wreath), fresh roses and miniature carnations, silver and white silk poinsettias (poinsettias may be spray painted if these colors are not available), floral water picks, wire cutters, silver star garland, decorative white sticks, hot glue gun, and glue sticks.

1. Use wire cutters to remove leaves from poinsettia stems; set aside. Referring to photo, arrange poinsettias by inserting wire stems into wreath. Bend wire stems around wreath to secure; trim ends if necessary.
2. Fill water picks with water; secure caps on picks.
3. Cut stems of roses and carnations desired lengths (approx. 4" to 6" lengths are best). Insert stems of flowers into water picks. Referring to photo, arrange fresh flowers by inserting water picks into wreath.
4. Referring to photo, glue poinsettia leaves and sticks to wreath.
5. Cut garland into approx. 6" lengths. Referring to photo, glue garland to wreath.

FABRIC TREES (Shown on page 76.)

For each tree, you will need silver lamé, silver metallic piping, craft batting, lightweight cardboard, one silver small star (see Metallic Cutouts, page 80; omit hanger), tracing paper, fabric glue, hot glue gun, and glue sticks.

1. Select desired size tree pattern from this page or page 83. (**Note:** Patterns have two cutting lines — one for cardboard/batting and one for fabric.) To make cardboard/batting pattern, place tracing paper over pattern and trace **inner** line only; cut out pattern. Repeat for fabric pattern, tracing **outer** line only.
2. With fabric pattern on right side of fabric, cut out three fabric shapes. Turn pattern over on right side of fabric; cut out three reversed fabric shapes.
3. Use cardboard/batting pattern to cut out six cardboard shapes. Repeat for six batting shapes.
4. For each tree shape, place a fabric shape right side down. Center one batting shape, then one cardboard shape, on fabric. At approx. ½" intervals, clip edges of fabric to within ⅛" of cardboard edges (**Fig. 1**).

Fig. 1

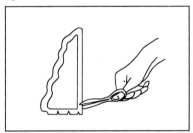

5. (**Note:** Leave corners unworked until Step 6.) Working along one side of tree shape, use fabric glue to adhere fabric to back of cardboard (**Fig. 2**). Pulling fabric taut, glue opposite side; repeat for bottom edge.

Fig. 2

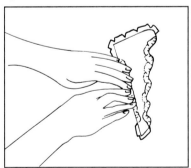

6. Apply fabric glue to corners of cardboard. Pinch excess fabric between fingers and press down into glue. Allow to dry, then clip excess fabric at corners. Repeat for a total of six tree shapes.

7. Hot glue piping along side and bottom edges of three tree shapes (**Fig. 3**). Match wrong sides of one tree shape to one reversed tree shape; hot glue wrong sides together. Repeat for remaining tree shapes.

Fig. 3

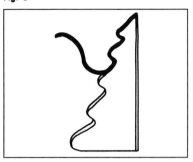

8. Referring to photo, hot glue straight edges of tree shapes together.
9. Hot glue star to top of tree.

SMALL TREE

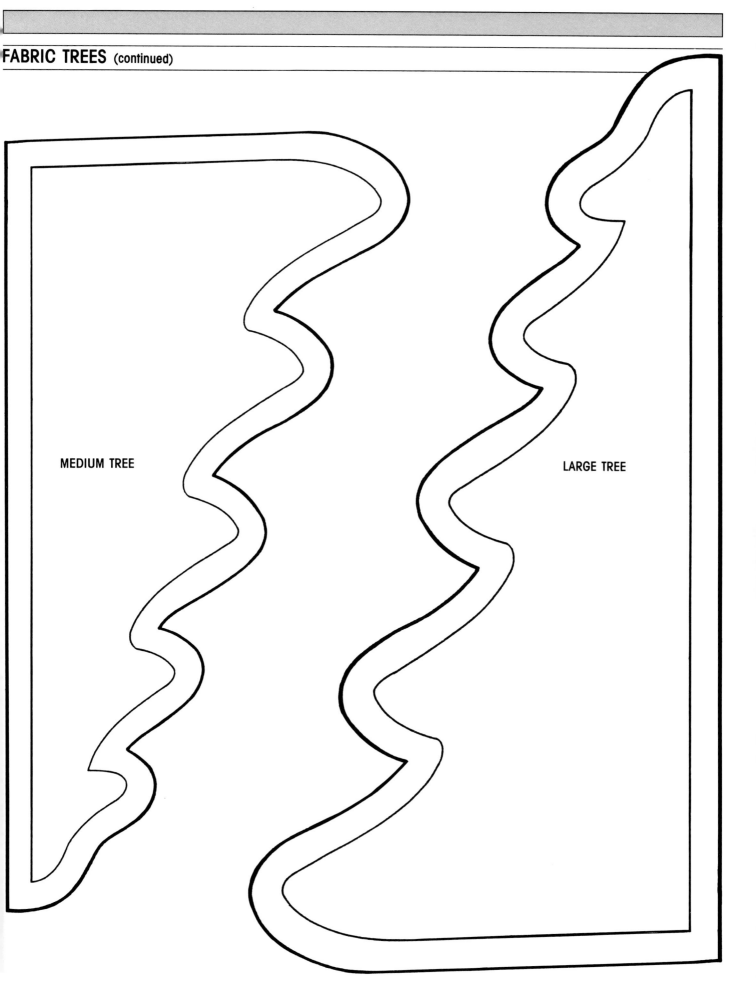

MEDIUM TREE

LARGE TREE

CHRISTMAS TABLE LINENS   (Shown on page 79.)

For Table Runner, you will need one 15½" x 44" (or desired size) piece of White Belfast Linen (32 ct), **Reindeer and Trees** design (chart on page 85), embroidery floss and beads (see color key, page 85), embroidery hoop (optional), #10 crewel needle or needle that will pass through beads, and white sewing thread.

1. Fold all edges of fabric under ½" and press; fold under ½" again and press.
2. For Hemstitch, use white sewing thread and begin working at lower left corner on wrong side of fabric. Bring thread over two fabric threads of hem and around two threads on fabric at top of hem (**Fig. 1**). (**Note:** It may be necessary to gather three threads together in the corners.) Work Hemstitch on all edges. When Hemstitch is complete, tack corners in place.

Fig. 1

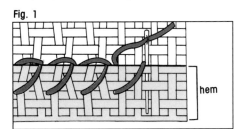

3. Following **Working on Linen**, page 157, center the design with bottom of design 2¼" from one short edge of fabric. Work design over two fabric threads, using 2 strands of floss for Cross Stitch. Repeat to work design on remaining short edge of fabric.
4. Attach beads as indicated on page 85; randomly place additional beads for "falling snow" (these are not shown on chart).

For Napkin, you will need one 17" x 17" (or desired size) piece of White Belfast Linen (32 ct), **Snowflake** design (chart on page 85), embroidery floss and beads (see color key, page 85), embroidery hoop (optional), #10 crewel needle or needle that will pass through beads, and white sewing thread.

1. Fold all edges of fabric under ½" and press; fold under ½" again and press.
2. For Hemstitch, see Table Runner, Step 2.
3. Following **Working on Linen**, page 157, center the design in one corner ¾" from edges of fabric. Work design over two fabric threads, using 2 strands of floss for Cross Stitch.
4. Attach beads as indicated on page 85.

For Mini Bag, you will need two 5" x 6½" (or desired size) pieces of White Belfast Linen (32 ct), one tree from **Reindeer and Trees** design (chart on page 85), embroidery floss and beads (see color key, page 85), embroidery hoop (optional), 28" each of ⅛"w white and pink ribbon, 28" of 1⁄16"w grey ribbon, #10 crewel needle or needle that will pass through beads, white sewing thread, and a small gift or decorative white sticks (optional).

1. On each fabric piece, fold one short edge under ¼" and press; fold under ¼" again and press (this will be the top of bag).
2. For Hemstitch, see Table Runner, Step 2, and begin working at left edge on wrong side of each fabric piece.

3. On one fabric piece, follow **Working on Linen**, page 157, and center the design with bottom of design 2" from bottom edge of fabric. Work design over two fabric threads, using 2 strands of floss for Cross Stitch.
4. Attach beads as indicated on page 85.
5. Matching right sides and leaving top edge open, use ½" seam allowance to sew fabric pieces together along sides and bottom edge. Trim seams and cut corner seam allowances diagonally. Turn right side out.
6. If desired, insert a small gift or decorative sticks into bag.
7. Referring to photo, tie ribbons around bag; knot ends as shown.

For Place Card, you will need one piece of White Belfast Linen (32 ct) 2"h and the width required for name (see Steps 1 and 2), **Alphabet** (chart on this page), embroidery floss and bead (see color key, page 85; omit bead if not working small snowflake), grid paper, craft glue, lightweight poster board, #10 crewel needle or needle that will pass through bead, and white sewing thread.

1. Use **Alphabet** to chart desired name on grid paper, leaving one square between letters. If small snowflake is desired, refer to photo for placement and chart snowflake (included in **Alphabet** chart) above name.
2. Count the number of squares in the name and divide by 16 (design will be stitched over two fabric threads on 32 count fabric). Add 1½" to the above figure and cut fabric the determined width and 2"h.
3. Following **Working on Linen**, page 157, center the design on fabric. Work design over two fabric threads, using 2 strands of floss for Cross Stitch, 1 for Backstitch, and 1 for French Knots.
4. Attach bead in snowflake as indicated on page 85.
5. Fringe fabric on all edges ¼".
6. Cut poster board 3"h and the width of stitched piece less ½". With 3" side of poster board folded in half, center and glue stitched piece to one side of poster board.

Continued on page 85.

ALPHABET

CHRISTMAS TABLE LINENS

(continued)

ATTACHING BEADS

Beads from Mill Hill Graphics, Inc., are placed over completed stitches. Beads are represented on the chart by a circle of color outlined in black. The color of bead to use is indicated on the color key under **Bead**.

Using one strand of white sewing thread, bring needle up at lower left corner of intersection of threads. Bring needle through bead and down in upper right corner of intersection of threads (**Fig. 1**).

Fig. 1

CHRISTMAS TABLE LINENS

X	DMC	B'ST	ANC.	COLOR
	414	✎	0399	grey
▦	415		0397	lt grey

BEAD*

◉	479K	White

* See **Attaching Beads** on this page.

REINDEER AND TREES (138w x 36h)

SNOWFLAKE (23w x 23h)

THE SHARING OF CHRISTMAS

Giving is one of the greatest joys of Christmas, and you want your gifts to be as special as the people who receive them. Gifts that are lovingly crafted by hand show how much you care, and they are sure to be appreciated and admired.

The gifts in this section are beautiful (and practical) ways to show your genuine love and affection. They are all easy to make — and easy on your budget. There are cozy afghans, fireplace accessories, a pillowcase for sweet dreamers, and an apron for that special hostess.

Even those friends who have ''everything'' will enjoy the gift baskets of delicious treats. You'll find something for everyone on your list — even some gifts that children can make.

This year, put something of yourself into all your gifts and share the excitement when each is received with joy. You'll have a merry Christmas, indeed.

FIRE
STARTER
GIFT
BASKET

Gift-giving at Christmastime doesn't have to be expensive or time consuming. Pinecones and paraffin are the two main ingredients in this gift basket for your friends with fireplaces. The pinecones are simply dipped in tinted paraffin and allowed to harden atop a paraffin base.

Dress up a plain basket with fabric or ribbon to hold the fire starters, include a bundle of long fireplace matches, and you have a gift that is decorative as well as practical. When your friends are warming by the fire, they'll know that gifts crafted by hand also warm hearts.

FIRE STARTER GIFT BASKET

You will need pinecones with approx. 2½ " dia. bases, paraffin, wax coloring chips (or crayons), scented oil for candles, candlewicks cut in 6" lengths, muffin tin, vegetable oil, double boiler or electric frying pan, large can for melting wax in frying pan, tongs, newspapers, desired basket to hold fire starters (we used a quarter-peck fruit basket), and fabric to decorate basket (optional).

1. CAUTION: Do not melt paraffin over an open flame or directly on burner. Cover work area with newspapers. Melt paraffin over hot water in double boiler or in a can placed in an electric frying pan filled with water. Add desired number of coloring chips and drops of scented oil.
2. Holding pinecones with tongs, dip cones in paraffin. Allow paraffin to harden.

3. Using vegetable oil, lightly oil muffin cups. Fill each cup half full with paraffin. Place one end of a wick in each cup, leaving other end free. Place a pinecone upright in each cup; allow paraffin to harden. Remove fire starters from cups.
4. Decorate basket as desired (we used strips of border-print fabric to decorate our basket).
5. Fill gift basket with fire starters and include a card with these instructions: Place several fire starters under logs and light wicks.

HOLIDAY FARE FOR YOUR FEATHERED FRIENDS

Christmas is a time for giving and sharing. So why not celebrate the season this year by sharing treats with the feathered friends in your neighborhood. Birdseed wreaths, made with refrigerated breadstick dough, can be hung from ribbon for the birds to enjoy. Enlist the aid of the neighborhood children to make and decorate a tree for the birds. In cold weather areas, birdseed can be mixed with lard and formed into balls to hang on the tree. Popcorn garlands and orange baskets filled with birdseed and raisins are two more types of holiday fare that will be greatly appreciated by your feathered friends.

BIRDSEED WREATHS

You will need one can of refrigerated breadstick dough, birdseed, one egg white, hot glue gun, glue sticks, and ¼ "w red satin ribbon.

1. Separate dough into individual pieces. Dip each piece in egg white and roll in birdseed, pressing seeds firmly into dough.
2. On lightly greased cookie sheet, form each piece into a heart shape. Pinch ends together at top. Bake as directed on can.
3. For hangers, cut ribbon desired lengths. Hot glue one end of each length to back of each wreath. Nail other end of ribbon to side of fence or tree.

BIRDSEED BALLS

You will need 1 cup lard, 2 cups birdseed, and jute for hanger.

1. In a bowl, mix lard and birdseed.
2. For each ball, cut an 8" length of jute and knot ends together in a double knot. Using approx.

½ cup of birdseed mixture, mold a ball around knot.
3. Tie a second knot at top of ball. Hang on a tree limb.

ORANGE BASKETS

For two orange baskets, you will need one orange, spoon, paring knife, permanent felt-tip pen, toothpick, raisins, birdseed, and 8" of jute for each hanger.

1. Cut orange in half. Scoop out orange pulp with spoon.
2. Referring to photo, use felt-tip pen to draw points around cut edge of each orange half. Using paring knife, cut away excess orange.
3. To hang orange baskets, use toothpick to make holes at opposite sides of each orange half. Thread jute through holes and knot each end on inside of orange baskets.
4. Fill orange baskets with raisins and birdseed. Hang on a tree limb.

COZY AFGHANS TO CROCHET

A handmade afghan is a gift that keeps on giving year after year. When you think of the many nights of cozy comfort these two beauties will bring, you will want to crochet one for every loved one on your list. Whether you make the Granny Ripple Afghan *(left)* or the Puff Stitch Afghan *(right)*, you'll discover that a handmade gift is both a pleasure to give and a pleasure to receive. Isn't that what gift-giving is all about?

GENERAL INSTRUCTIONS

ABBREVIATIONS

ch(s)	chain(s)
dc	double crochet(s)
LDC	Long double crochet
mm	millimeters
sc	single crochet(s)
sp	space
st(s)	stitch(es)
YO	yarn over

★ — work instructions following ★ as many **more** times as indicated in addition to the first time.

† to † — work all instructions from first † to second † **as many** times as specified.

( ) or [ ] — work enclosed instructions **as many** times as specified by the number immediately following **or** work all enclosed instructions in the stitch or space indicated **or** contains explanatory remarks.

TASSEL

Cut a piece of cardboard 7" square. Wind yarn loosely and evenly around cardboard. When cardboard is filled, cut yarn across one end; repeat as needed. Hold 5 strands together and fold in half. With **wrong** side of Afghan facing and using a crochet hook, draw folded ends through space or stitch specified in instructions, forming a loop; pull loose ends through loop and draw knot up tightly (**Figs. 1a & b**). Continue until all Tassels have been attached. Lay Afghan flat on hard surface and trim ends evenly.

Fig. 1a

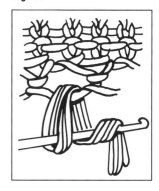

Fig. 1b

90

GRANNY RIPPLE AFGHAN

Size: Approximately 48" x 60"

MATERIALS

"Berella 4" by Bernat (100 gram balls)
(approximately 250 meters (240 yards) per
ball) OR any equivalent worsted weight yarn
that will work to the specified gauge
- A - 3 balls #8879 Pale Sea Green
- B - 5 balls #8877 Medium Sea Green
- C - 5 balls #8940 Natural

Leisure Arts crochet hook, size K (7.00 mm) **or**
size needed for gauge
Yarn needle

GAUGE: 1 pattern repeat (from point to point) = 6"
DO NOT HESITATE TO CHANGE HOOK SIZE
TO OBTAIN CORRECT GAUGE.

Note: To change colors, finish off existing color
and join new color with slip st in last st worked.

STRIPE SEQUENCE

Work one row **each** with:
A, B, C, A, B, C, A;
Work 4 rows with B.
Work one row **each** with:
A, C, B, A, C, B, A;
Work 4 rows with C.
Repeat these 22 rows for Stripe Sequence.

PATTERN STITCHES

Cluster: (YO, insert hook in st or sp and draw up
a loop, YO and draw through 2 loops on hook) 3
times, YO and draw through all 4 loops on hook.

**Long Double Crochet Group, abbreviated LDC
Group:** Work dc in sp before next group, YO, insert
hook in center st of group below same sp and
pull up a loop even with last dc worked **(Fig. 1a)**,
complete as a dc, dc in same sp as last dc
worked **(Fig. 1b)**.

Fig. 1a

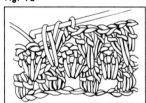

Fig. 1b

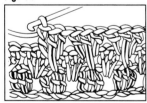

Long Double Crochet Shell, abbreviated LDC Shell:
Work dc in next Shell, † YO, insert hook in Shell
below same Shell and pull up a loop even with
last dc worked, complete as a dc **(Fig. 2a)** †,
(dc, ch 3, dc) in same Shell as last dc worked,
repeat from † to † once, dc in same Shell as last
dc worked **(Fig. 2b)**.

Fig. 2a

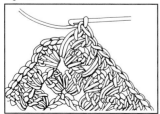

Fig. 2b

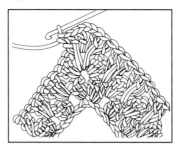

**Long Double Crochet Cluster, abbreviated LDC
Cluster:** YO, insert hook in sp before next Cluster
and pull up a loop, YO and draw through 2 loops
on hook, YO, insert hook in center st of group
below same sp and pull up a loop, YO and draw
through 2 loops on hook, YO, insert hook in same
sp as first loop drawn up and pull up a loop, YO
and draw through 2 loops on hook, YO and draw
through all 4 loops on hook.

With Pale Sea Green ch 230 **loosely**.

Row 1: 3 Dc in sixth ch from hook, skip 2 chs,
(3 dc in next ch, skip 2 chs) twice, (3 dc, ch 3,
3 dc) in next ch **(Shell made)**, skip 2 chs, (3 dc in
next ch, skip 2 chs) 3 times, ★ work Cluster in
next ch, skip 4 chs, work Cluster in next ch, skip 2
chs, (3 dc in next ch, skip 2 chs) 3 times, work
Shell in next ch, skip 2 chs, (3 dc in next ch, skip
2 chs) 3 times; repeat from ★ 6 times **more**, dc
in last ch.

Row 2: Ch 3 **(counts as first dc, now and
throughout)**, turn; skip first group, 3 dc in sp
before next group, (skip next group, 3 dc in sp
before next group) twice, work Shell in next Shell
(ch-3 sp), (3 dc in sp before next group, skip next
group) 3 times, ★ work Cluster in sp before next
Cluster, skip next 2 Clusters, work Cluster in sp
before next group, (skip next group, 3 dc in sp
before next group) 3 times, work Shell in next
Shell, (3 dc in sp before next group, skip next
group) 3 times; repeat from ★ 6 times **more**, dc
in last dc.

Row 3: Ch 3, turn; skip first group, work LDC
Group, (skip next group, work LDC Group) twice,
work LDC Shell, work LDC Group, (skip next group,
work LDC Group) twice, ★ work LDC Cluster, skip
next 2 Clusters, work LDC Cluster in sp before next
group, (skip next group, work LDC Group) 3 times,
work LDC Shell, (work LDC Group, skip next
group) 3 times; repeat from ★ 6 times **more**, dc
in last dc.

Rows 4-7: Repeat Rows 2 and 3, twice.
Rows 8-13: Repeat Row 2, 6 times.
Row 14: Repeat Row 3.
Repeat Rows 4-14 for pattern until Afghan
measures approximately 60" from beginning,
ending by working Row 7; finish off.

FINISHING

Make Tassels **(see General Instructions)** using
10 strands of A; attach between Clusters and at
each Shell.
Weave in all yarn ends.

PUFF STITCH AFGHAN

Size: Approximately 48" x 60"

MATERIALS

"Berella 4" by Bernat (100 gram balls) -
16 #8879 Pale Sea Green (approximately
250 meters (240 yards) per ball) OR any
equivalent worsted weight yarn that will work
to the specified gauge
Crochet hook, size N (9.00 mm) **or** size needed
for gauge
Yarn needle

GAUGE: Working double strand, 7 dc = 3"
DO NOT HESITATE TO CHANGE HOOK SIZE
TO OBTAIN CORRECT GAUGE.

Note: Entire Afghan is worked holding two strands
of yarn together.

Ch 142 **loosely**.
Row 1: Dc in fourth ch from hook and in each ch
across: 140 sts.
Row 2: Ch 3 **(counts as first dc, now and
throughout)**, turn; dc in next dc and in each dc
across.
Row 3: Ch 1, turn; sc in first 2 dc, in same dc as
last sc work Puff St as follows: (YO, insert hook
and pull up a loop) 3 times in same dc **(Fig. 3a)**,
YO and draw through 6 loops on hook, YO and
draw through both loops on hook **(Puff St made,
Fig. 3b)**, skip next dc, ★ (sc, work Puff St) in next
dc, skip next dc; repeat from ★ across to last dc,
dc in last dc: 69 Puff Sts.

Fig. 3a

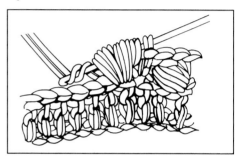

Fig. 3b

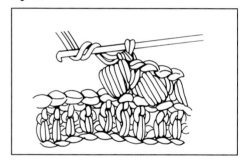

Row 4: Ch 1, turn; sc in first dc, (sc, work Puff St)
in each sc across to last sc, dc in last sc:
69 Puff Sts.
Rows 5 and 6: Ch 3, turn; dc in next st and in
each st across: 140 dc.
Row 7: Ch 4 **(counts as first dc plus ch 1)**, turn;
skip next dc, dc in next dc, ★ ch 1, skip next dc,
dc in next dc; repeat from ★ across to last dc, dc
in last dc: 71 dc.
Row 8: Ch 3, turn; dc in next dc and in each
ch-1 sp and dc across: 140 dc.
Repeat Rows 2-8 for pattern until Afghan
measures approximately 47½" from beginning,
ending by working Row 6.

Edging: Ch 1, turn; 3 sc in first dc, sc in each dc
across to last dc, 3 sc in last dc; working in end
of rows, sc evenly across; working in free loops of
beginning ch, 3 sc in first ch, sc in each ch
across to last ch, 3 sc in last ch; working in end
of rows, sc evenly across; join with slip st to first
sc, finish off.

FINISHING

Make Tassels **(see General Instructions)**; attach in
every other sc along both ends.
Weave in all yarn ends.

JOY APRON

Simple machine sewing turns a mail-order apron into a darling holiday accent for that special host or hostess on your Christmas list. Because appliquéing these simple shapes is so quick and easy, you'll want to make several for gifts (and keep one for yourself). The goofy reindeer adds a touch of whimsy to the cheerful holiday message: Joy — to the world!

JOY APRON

You will need one chef's apron, 5" square of tan cotton fabric, 8" x 6" piece of red cotton fabric, 4" x 6" piece of brown acrylic felt, 3½" of ⅜"w red grosgrain ribbon, 3½" of ⅝"w green grosgrain ribbon, ½" dia. red pom-pom for nose, two ¼" dia. black beads (or buttons) for eyes, fusible webbing, reusable pressing sheet (available at fabric stores for use with fusible webbing), tracing paper, and thread to match fabrics.

(**Note:** When instructions indicate machine appliqué, use a narrow zigzag stitch and a short stitch length.)

1. Trace the following patterns onto tracing paper along solid and dashed lines: "J," "Y," reindeer head, and antlers. Cut out pattern pieces.

2. Using fusible webbing and pressing sheet (follow manufacturer's instructions), fuse webbing to wrong side of fabrics and to one side of felt piece.
3. Pin patterns on fabrics as follows and cut out pieces: red fabric for J and Y, tan fabric for reindeer head, and brown felt for antlers.
4. Refer to photo and pattern for placement of pieces. With webbed side down, fuse pieces to apron.
5. Center and fuse red ribbon to green ribbon. Using fusible webbing and pressing sheet (follow manufacturer's instructions), fuse webbing to green ribbon. Referring to pattern for placement, trim ends of ribbons even with sides of head. Fuse green ribbon to reindeer head.
6. Using thread to match fabrics, machine appliqué outer edges of all pieces.
7. Attach pom-pom and beads to reindeer where indicated on pattern.

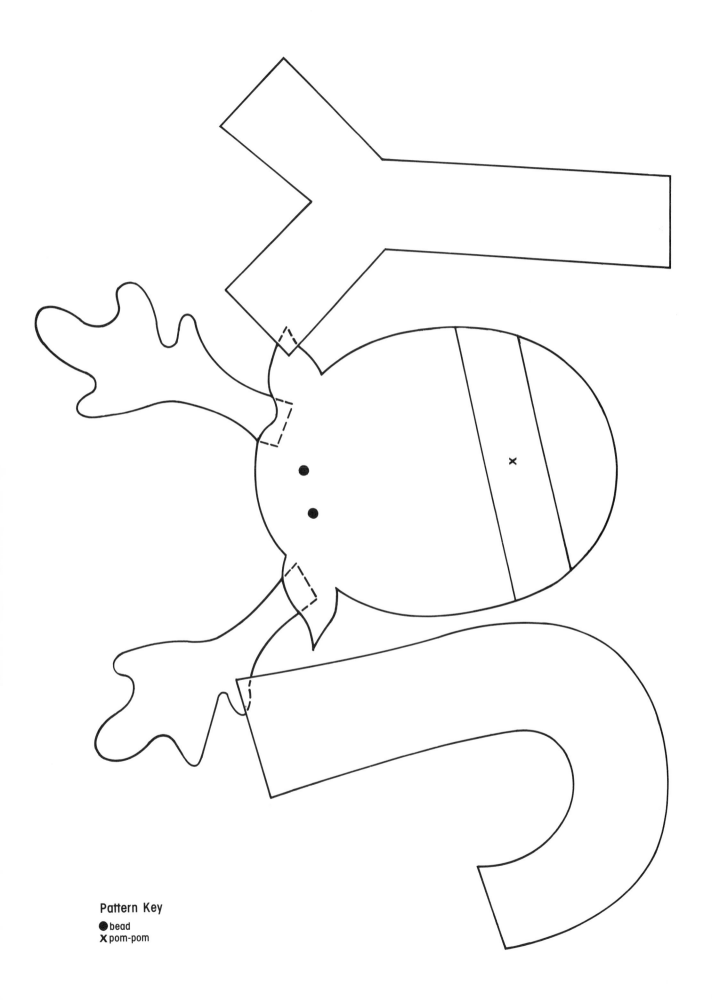

Pattern Key

● bead
X pom-pom

93

BATH
WRAPS

What to give to the Joneses? How about his and hers bath wraps — a perfectly practical gift for that hard-to-buy-for couple on your list. Fashioned from bath towels, they are simple to make. Appliqué a sea horse on his. Put a seashell appliqué on hers and trim it with ribbon and eyelet. For an extra touch, fill a basket with coordinating bath accessories and sachets made from the seashell pattern.

BATH WRAPS

For Woman's Wrap, you will need one approx. 50" x 27" bath towel, 5"w pre-gathered eyelet the length of towel plus 1", ⅞"w grosgrain ribbon the length of towel plus 1", one 7" strip of Velcro® fastener, 20" of 1"w elastic for an average size woman (adjust for other sizes), one 6" square of fabric for shell appliqué, fusible webbing, reusable pressing sheet (available at fabric stores for use with fusible webbing), desired colors of thread, and tracing paper.

1. To form casing for elastic, fold one long edge of towel 1½" to wrong side. Beginning and ending 7½" from short edges, sew 1¼" from fold. Insert elastic in casing and securely sew each end of elastic to towel 7½" from short edges. Complete casing on each side of elastic by sewing from elastic to short edge of towel 1¼" from fold.

2. With right side of towel up, sew one piece of Velcro® fastener (soft side) along ungathered section of casing as shown in **Fig. 1**. With wrong side of towel up, sew remaining piece of Velcro® fastener (firm side) along ungathered section of casing as shown in **Fig. 2**.

Fig. 1

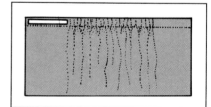

Fig. 2

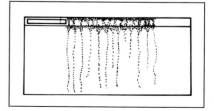

3. To trim lower edge of towel, fold short edges of eyelet under ½" and press. With right sides up and with towel on top, sew eyelet to lower edge of towel. Fold short edges of ribbon under ½" and press. On right side of towel, sew both long edges of ribbon to lower edge of towel.

4. For shell appliqué, trace shell pattern onto tracing paper and cut out. Using fusible webbing and pressing sheet (follow manufacturer's instructions), fuse webbing to wrong side of 6" square of fabric. Center pattern on right side of fabric and cut out. Use a pencil to lightly draw detail lines on shell. With right side of towel facing up and referring to photo, position shell on lower right-hand side of towel. With webbed side down, fuse shell to towel. Using a narrow zigzag stitch and a short stitch length, machine appliqué shell to towel (including detail lines on shell).

For Man's Wrap, you will need one approx. 50" x 27" bath towel, one 7" strip of Velcro® fastener, 24" of 1"w elastic for an average size man (adjust for other sizes), one 5" x 7" piece of fabric for sea horse appliqué, fusible webbing, reusable pressing sheet (available at fabric stores for use with fusible webbing), black embroidery floss, desired colors of thread, and tracing paper.

1. To form casing and to attach Velcro® fastener, follow Steps 1 and 2 of Woman's Wrap, page 94.

2. For sea horse appliqué, trace only the sea horse from pattern onto tracing paper and cut out. Using 5" x 7" piece of fabric and following Step 4 of Woman's Wrap, machine appliqué sea horse to towel. Use black embroidery floss to work French Knot for eye. For coral, it is easier to create your own arrangement than to duplicate pattern. Using desired color of thread and a narrow zigzag stitch, machine appliqué coral referring to pattern for placement.

SHELL SACHETS

For each sachet, you will need two 6" squares of fabric, polyester fiberfill, cotton ball, scented oil, thread to match fabric, fabric marking pencil, small crochet hook, and tracing paper.

1. Use shell pattern and follow **Transferring Patterns** and **Sewing Shapes**, page 157, to make desired number of sachets.

2. Stuff with fiberfill. Place a few drops of oil on cotton ball and insert in sachet; sew final closure by hand.

3. Referring to pattern and working through all thicknesses, work detail lines of shell using a small running stitch.

CHRISTMAS SAMPLER

A cross stitch sampler, lovingly rendered by hand, is a gift of timeless beauty that is destined to become a family heirloom. The birth of the Christ Child is commemorated in this exquisite design. The subtle shading and the lovely linen fabric allow it to blend with any home decor. Since it's much too pretty to display only at Christmas, it will serve all year long as a gentle reminder of our heritage.

CHRISTMAS SAMPLER

You will need one 12" x 15" piece of Cream Belfast Linen (32 ct), embroidery floss (see color key, page 97), embroidery hoop (optional), and desired frame.

1. Following **Working on Linen**, page 157, center design on fabric. Work design over two fabric threads, using 2 strands of floss for Cross Stitch, 2 for Satin Stitch (see page 97), 1 for Backstitch, and 1 for French Knots.
2. Frame sampler as desired (we used a custom frame).

CHRISTMAS SAMPLER
(79w x 127h)

X	DMC	SATIN STITCH	B'ST	COLOR
O	ecru			ecru
V	223			pink
⊙	224	☐		lt pink
S	316			mauve
★	524			green
☐	645		╱	grey
X	841			beige
△	842	☐		lt beige
	926		╱	blue
✚	927	☐		lt blue
C	3032			tan
☆	3046		╱	gold
•	926	blue French Knot		
•	3046	gold French Knot		

*See Figs. 1 & 2 for working Satin Stitch.

CHRISTMAS SAMPLER (79w x 127h)

Aida 11	7¼" x 11⅝"
Aida 14	5¾" x 9⅛"
Aida 18	4½" x 7⅛"
Hardanger 22	3⅝" x 5⅞"

Satin Stitch On Linen: Come up at 1; working over six fabric threads, go down at 2. Come up at 3 and go down at 4 **(Fig. 1)**. Repeat pattern for each row **(Fig. 2)**.

Fig. 1

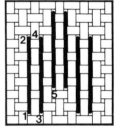

Fig. 2

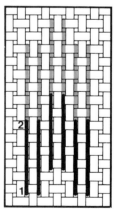

SEASON'S GREETINGS DOORMAT

Christmastime calls for special messages to inspire friendliness and good cheer. This handsomely painted message is delivered by Father Christmas himself. Decorating this cotton rug is easy with the help of a simple painting technique and packaged lettering stencils. When your Christmas gifts are handmade, they always send a special message. Season's Greetings!

SEASON'S GREETINGS DOORMAT

You will need one 24" x 36" cotton rug; hot-iron fabric transfer pencil; water-soluble fabric marking pen; tracing paper; 2½" Roman lettering stencils; medium-size stencil brush; #4 flat paintbrush; red, white, green, flesh, lt grey, dk grey, and black acrylic paint, and pressing cloth.

1. Trace patterns (including all detail lines) for Santa, holly, and heart (used as berries) onto tracing paper. For Santa pattern only, turn pattern over and use fabric transfer pencil to draw over lines on back of pattern. Cut out holly and heart patterns.
2. For placement of Santa, measure approx. 7" from top and bottom edges of rug and 6½" from left edge. Follow transfer pencil manufacturer's instructions to transfer Santa to rug.
3. For placement of phrase, measure approx. 12" from top edge of rug. Beginning 2" from Santa, use water-soluble fabric marking pen and a ruler to draw a line approx. 15" long. Measure 4" down from first line; beginning 2" from Santa, draw another line approx. 20" long. Using lettering stencils and following manufacturer's instructions for letter placement, stencil "SEASON'S GREETINGS" with red acrylic paint.
4. Referring to photo for placement and using fabric marking pen, draw around holly and heart patterns at corners of rug and at end of phrase.
5. Referring to photo for colors, paint designs.
6. Allow paint to dry thoroughly. Remove any marking pen lines following manufacturer's instructions. To make designs permanent, use a pressing cloth and press painted areas with a hot iron.

PAINTED SHAKER BOXES

American Christmas folk art is uniquely displayed on a stack of Shaker boxes. The perfect accent for country decor, these boxes make an unusual holiday gift that will be treasured for years to come.

Part of the charm of folk art is its simple, childlike quality. This makes it a great project for beginners. Follow the patterns for the basic elements and the photograph for color; then fill in with stars and snowflakes.

PAINTED SHAKER BOXES

You will need one each of the following diameter wooden Shaker boxes: 5", 6", and 6½"; 1"w disposable foam brush; #1 round and #4 flat paintbrushes; tracing paper; white transfer paper; ballpoint pen that does not write; transparent tape; water-base satin varnish; and dk blue, yellow, white, green, dk grey, burgundy, brown, black, beige, flesh, and red or desired colors of acrylic paint.

1. Trace patterns onto tracing paper.
2. Using foam brush, apply two coats of dk blue paint to all boxes. Allow to dry.
3. Using pattern #1 and 6½" dia. box, place transfer paper, coated side down, behind pattern and position on side of box. Tape edges of pattern and transfer paper in place.

4. Using a ballpoint pen that does not write, lightly draw over the pattern. (**Note:** Do not press hard; it could indent the wood or tear the tracing paper.)
5. Repeat Steps 3 and 4 to transfer pattern #2 onto 6" dia. box and pattern #3 onto 5" dia. box.
6. Using white paint and flat paintbrush, paint snowy ground on 6½" dia. box. (**Note:** If desired, freehand paint hills and trees to extend design around back of box.) Allow to dry.
7. Using round paintbrush and referring to photo for colors, paint designs.
8. Referring to photo as necessary, freehand paint snowflakes and stars.
9. Allow boxes to dry thoroughly. Apply one coat of varnish to boxes.

TORN PAPER GREETING CARDS

TORN PAPER GREETING CARDS

This holiday project is a great group activity for family and friends.

You will need desired colors of construction paper, tracing paper, glue, and string (for mitten card).

1. For each card, fold one 8½" x 11" sheet of construction paper in half matching short edges.
2. Trace desired patterns onto tracing paper; cut out.
3. Referring to photo for colors, draw around patterns on construction paper.
4. (**Note:** Some designs are cut out and others are torn. On the pattern pieces, black lines are cutting lines and grey lines are tearing lines.)

Using lines as guides, carefully cut or tear out shapes.
5. For mitten card, refer to photo and lay a 10" length of string on card for clothesline. Glue ends to back of card. Cut tiny strips of construction paper to resemble clothespins. Glue mittens and clothespins to card.
6. For sheep card, glue sheep and wreath to card. Tear small pieces of red construction paper to resemble berries. Glue to wreath.
7. For snowman card, cut a piece of white construction paper to fit bottom of card. Tear top edge of construction paper to resemble ground; glue to bottom of card. Glue snowman pieces to card.

Many Christmas memories are tied to the tradition of giving and receiving Christmas cards. When the cards are made by children, these memories become all the more precious.

Little fingers will be busy tearing simple shapes and gluing them to construction paper cards. Most of the shapes for the cards are torn rather than cut with scissors. Three designs are included to get the kids started, but when little imaginations get in the holiday spirit, all sorts of designs are likely.

Start a new tradition in your family and begin making this year's memories today.

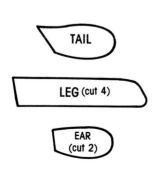
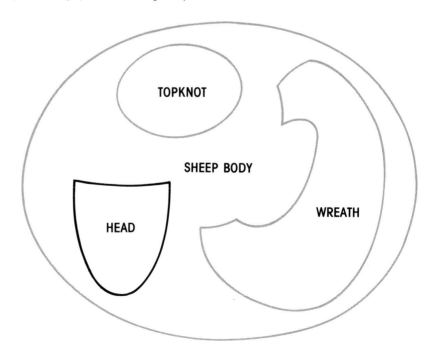

Continued from page 102.)

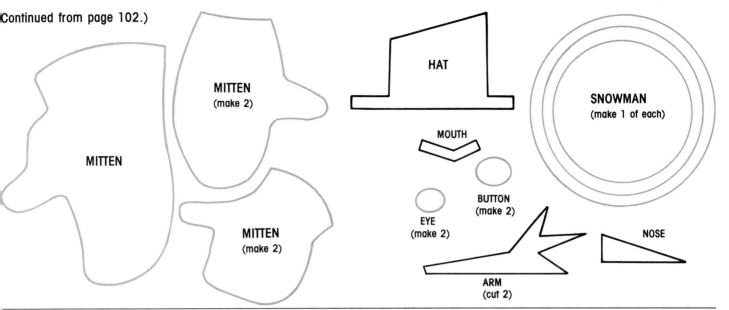

MITTEN

MITTEN
(make 2)

HAT

SNOWMAN
(make 1 of each)

MITTEN
(make 2)

MOUTH

EYE
(make 2)

BUTTON
(make 2)

NOSE

ARM
(cut 2)

SNOWMAN PICTURE MAT

Crafting Christmas gifts is always more fun when children are involved. This Christmas, why not let your little ones give pictures of themselves in mats that they have made. Mom does the cutting and outlining, and the little one does the coloring. The result: Mom and child make a wonderful memory, and Grandma receives a treasure.

SNOWMAN PICTURE MAT

You will need one 5" x 7" free-standing Lucite™ frame; one 5" x 7" piece of desired color construction paper; chalk, colored pencils, or crayons; black permanent felt-tip pen; tracing paper; white transfer paper (if using dark construction paper) or graphite transfer paper (if using light construction paper); photograph; blunt pencil; transparent tape, and hair spray or fixative (if using chalk).

Continued on page 104.

(Continued from page 103.)

1. Trace pattern onto tracing paper.
2. Use transfer paper and blunt pencil to transfer pattern to construction paper.
3. Refer to photo for colors and use chalk, colored pencils, or crayons to color mat.
4. If using chalk, spray paper with hair spray or fixative to prevent smearing.
5. Referring to photo, use pen to outline and define design.
6. Cut out center of mat as indicated on pattern.
7. Center and tape photograph to wrong side of mat; insert in frame.

CUT OUT

PAINTED PILLOWCASE

Imagine how delighted the little dreamer on your list will be with his or her very own personalized pillowcase. Using a simple painting technique, you can transform a plain pillowcase into a special handmade gift that any little lamb would love to dream on.

PAINTED PILLOWCASE

You will need one pillowcase; tracing paper; graphite transfer paper; red, white, and black acrylic paint; #3 round, #10 flat, and #2 script liner paintbrushes; black permanent felt-tip pen with fine point (optional); blunt pencil; pressing cloth, and paper towels.

1. Wash, dry, and press pillowcase.
2. Trace sheep pattern onto tracing paper.
3. (**Note:** We used the heart necklace on only one sheep.) Referring to photo for placement, use transfer paper and a blunt pencil to transfer pattern to pillowcase. Repeat for a total of four sheep.
4. Place a double thickness of paper towels inside pillowcase under area to be painted. Refer to photo for colors and paint each sheep in the following order: face, legs, body, ear, and heart. Allow to dry thoroughly. Paint white lines on legs using script liner paintbrush.
5. Referring to photo, paint numbers and desired name using black paint and script liner paintbrush or pen. Allow to dry thoroughly.
6. To make design permanent, use a pressing cloth and press painted areas with a hot iron. (**Note:** To launder pillowcase, turn inside out and hand wash. Turn right side out and allow to air dry; press with a warm iron.)

AN ASSORTMENT OF SCENTS

In the air there's a feeling of Christmas, and the scents of the season add to the holiday spirit. We have collected a sampling of seasonal scents to bring fresh ideas to your gift-giving. A stroll through the winter woods and a handful of spices from the kitchen provide most of the materials.

In our array, you will find a potpourri made especially for simmering, scented candles in Santa shapes, a bundle of cinnamon sticks tied with a cheery ribbon, and two other potpourris. A mason jar makes a great container for the small potpourri, and a large basket is impressive for the jumbo version. Fill a bag with simmering potpourri and attach to a simmer pot.

Whether you fill your gift baskets with an assortment of scents or choose just one, your friends will think your gifts are truly "scentsational."

SCENTED SANTA CANDLES

For each pair of Santa candles, you will need paraffin, red wax coloring chips (or red crayons), scented oil for candles, candlewick, two identical Santa candy molds (we used 3" molds), vegetable oil, double boiler or electric frying pan, large can for melting wax in frying pan, newspapers, craft knife, and modeling clay.

1. **Caution: Do not melt paraffin over an open flame or directly on burner.** Cover work area with newspapers. Melt paraffin over hot water in double boiler or in a can placed in an electric frying pan filled with water. Add desired number of coloring chips and 1 — 2 drops of scented oil.
2. Using vegetable oil, lightly oil molds. Prop molds so they will be level. Cut wick the length of both molds plus 8". Pour melted wax into molds. Center and place wick along backs of molds, leaving approx. 7" of wick between tops of molds and ½" extending at bottoms of molds. To secure wick, press small pieces of modeling clay over wick at tops and bottoms of molds. Allow paraffin to harden. (**Note:** As paraffin hardens, it will shrink in size.)
3. Add more paraffin to fill molds. Allow paraffin to harden.
4. Remove Santas from molds and trim any uneven edges with craft knife. Trim wicks at bases of candles.

SIMMERING POTPOURRI

For potpourri, you will need one 1 oz. can cinnamon sticks (broken into small pieces), one 1.12 oz. can whole cloves, one 1.25 oz. can whole allspice, and two potpourri bags (instructions below).

For each potpourri bag, you will need two 5" x 7½" pieces of brown linen or desired fabric (a type that will ravel easily), thread to match fabric, and 22" of 3-ply jute.

1. Mix cinnamon pieces, cloves, and allspice.
2. To make each bag, place right sides of fabric pieces together. Leaving one short edge open and using ½" seam allowance, sew fabric pieces together along sides and bottom edge. Trim seams and cut corner seam allowances diagonally.
3. Turn bag right side out; fringe top edge ½".
4. Place 5 tablespoons of potpourri in each bag and tie with jute.
5. Attach the following instructions to potpourri bag: Place one heaping tablespoon of potpourri and ½ cup water in simmer pot. Heat mixture in simmer pot following manufacturer's instructions.

MASON JAR POTPOURRI

You will need eucalyptus, clusters of canella berries, sweet gum balls, small pinecones, fresh pine needles, cedar chips, bay leaves, cinnamon sticks (broken into pieces), desired scent of essential oil, and mason jar with tight-fitting lid.

1. Mix ingredients for potpourri and place in jar. Add desired amount of essential oil. Secure lid on jar. Place jar in a cool, dark, dry place for two weeks. Every few days, shake jar to mix contents.
2. Remove lid on jar to enjoy the delightful scent.

JUMBO POTPOURRI

You will need assorted sizes of pinecones, lotus pods, balsa wood cutouts, desired scent of essential oil, large plastic bag, one basket, and a piece of plastic wrap to line basket.

1. Mix ingredients and place in plastic bag. Add desired amount of essential oil. Close bag and allow contents to sit for two weeks, shaking bag every few days to mix contents. Add more oil as necessary.
2. Line basket with plastic wrap to prevent oil from seeping through basket and damaging any surfaces. Add potpourri to basket.

COOKIE PIZZAS

This fun-loving trio of teens loves to combine tastes and talents to create their own special Christmas gifts. This year they are making cookie pizzas, a gift they know is sure to please teachers and friends alike.

Refrigerated cookie dough serves as the crust. A variety of toppings includes nuts, chocolate chips, cherries, and whatever else these holiday imaginations concoct. Melted almond bark looks like cheese when drizzled on top. What fun!

COOKIE PIZZAS

For four 8" cookie pizzas, you will need one (20-ounce) roll refrigerated peanut butter cookie dough, almond bark, peanuts, maraschino cherries, semisweet chocolate chips, 8" round cake pan (cookie pizzas are baked one at a time), non-stick vegetable spray, wire rack, lightweight cardboard, four 9" pie boxes (available at bakeries), and ribbon to decorate boxes.

1. Using the bottom of the cake pan as a pattern, draw four circles on cardboard; cut out and set aside.
2. Spray cake pan with vegetable spray until well coated.
3. Divide cookie dough into 4 equal parts.
4. With floured hands, press one-fourth of dough into cake pan. Bake in preheated 350 degree oven for 8 to 10 minutes. Remove from pan and cool on wire rack. Repeat for a total of four cookies.
5. Place cookies on cardboard circles. Drain cherries and cut into halves. Referring to photo, decorate tops of cookies with cherries, peanuts, and chocolate chips.
6. Melt almond bark following package directions. Drizzle almond bark over cookies.
7. Place cookie pizzas in pie boxes and tie boxes with ribbon.

FLAVORFUL CHEESE SPREADS

Cream cheese, spiked with herbs and other goodies, brings to mind old-fashioned kitchen gardens. You start with one basic cheese spread. By adding different flavorings to each portion, you create three totally different spreads. What a time-saver!

Clay pots (3" diameter) make unique gift containers and really look authentic when staked with cross stitched labels. Just one pot of cheese makes a nice gift, but three are great, especially when nestled in a tray filled with oyster cracker "pebbles."

CHEESE SPREADS

BASIC SPREAD

    2 (8-ounce) packages cream cheese,
         softened
    ½ cup sour cream
    3 tablespoons mayonnaise

Beat cheese; add sour cream and mayonnaise. Whip until smooth. Basic Spread will make one each of the following recipes.
Yield: 2⅔ cups

GARLIC
    1½ teaspoons garlic salt
    1 teaspoon Fines Herbs
    ⅛ teaspoon Tabasco® sauce
    1 cup Basic Spread
Mix all ingredients. Fill container and sprinkle with herbs. Serve with assorted crackers.

CHEESE
    ⅓ cup Parmesan cheese, grated
    ¾ teaspoon onion salt
    1 teaspoon Worcestershire sauce
    1 cup Basic Spread
Mix all ingredients. Fill container and sprinkle with Parmesan cheese. Serve with assorted crackers or wedges of red apple.

ALMOND
    ¼ cup butter, softened
    ¼ cup sugar
    ⅛ cup golden raisins
    ⅛ cup slivered almonds, lightly toasted
    ⅔ cup Basic Spread
Mix all ingredients. Fill container and sprinkle with raisins or almonds. Serve with assorted fruits or crackers.

CHEESE LABELS

For each label, you will need one 2" x 3" piece of perforated paper, desired color of floss, #24 tapestry needle, craft stick, craft glue, and small piece of manila folder for backing.

1. (**Note:** Perforated paper has a right and wrong side. The right side is smoother and stitching should be done on this side. Hold paper flat while stitching.) Center and stitch desired design, using three strands of floss for Cross Stitch and two strands for Backstitch.

2. Cut out label following grey line on chart. From small piece of manila folder, cut backing piece slightly smaller than stitched piece.

3. Glue backing piece to wrong side of stitched piece.

4. Glue craft stick to wrong side of label.

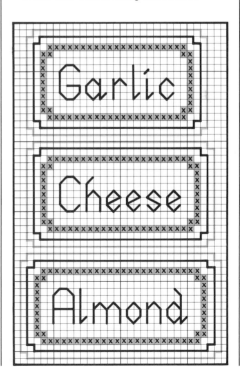

HERB BREAD

Sharing with friends is what Christmas is all about. A loaf of homemade bread is a special way of saying you care during this season of sharing.

A loaf of home-baked, braided Herb Bread, accompanied by a crock of Basil Butter, is a truly impressive gift — not only because it is delicious, but because it says you care enough to take the time.

HERB BREAD

    1 package active dry yeast
    3 tablespoons sugar
    ¼ cup warm water
    6 cups flour
    2 teaspoons salt
    2 tablespoons basil
    1 tablespoon dried parsley
    4 eggs
    2 tablespoons vegetable oil
    1¼ cups warm milk
       Basil Butter (recipe follows)

Stir yeast and sugar into warm water; let stand 5 minutes.

In large mixing bowl, combine 4 cups flour, salt, basil, and parsley.

Separate 1 egg (reserve egg yolk). Add remaining 3 eggs to egg white and beat with fork until frothy. Stir in yeast mixture, oil, and milk.

Stir liquid mixture into flour mixture and beat until smooth. Stir in remaining flour to make a stiff dough.

Turn dough onto a lightly floured surface and knead for 8 to 10 minutes or until smooth and elastic. Place in greased bowl, turning once to grease top. Cover with a towel and let rise until double in bulk (about 1 hour). Punch down dough and let rise until double again (about 1 hour).

Divide dough into three equal parts; roll each part into a rope about 18 inches long. Braid ropes and place on greased baking sheet. Press each end firmly together; tuck ends under loaf to seal. Cover and let rise until double in bulk (about 1 hour).

Beat reserved egg yolk with fork and brush over braid. Bake in a preheated 375 degree oven for 40 to 45 minutes or until light golden brown. Remove from baking sheet and cool on wire rack. Serve with Basil Butter.

Yield: 1 braided loaf

BASIL BUTTER

    1 cup butter, softened
    3 tablespoons basil

In mixing bowl, whip together butter and basil. Chill before serving.

RASPBERRY LIQUEUR AND CREAM PUFFS

Gifts that taste good are gifts of good taste. A bottle of homemade Raspberry Liqueur makes a tasteful gift that anyone would enjoy. For an extra special treat, pack a gift basket with a pair of liqueur glasses and a bag of Cream Puffs. Later, when the Cream Puffs are filled with ice cream and topped with Raspberry Liqueur Sauce, and the liqueur is being savored, your friends will be heralding your gift of good taste!

RASPBERRY LIQUEUR

Raspberry Liqueur is delicious served over vanilla or chocolate ice cream. We filled our Cream Puffs with creamy vanilla ice cream and topped them with Raspberry Liqueur Sauce.

- 2 (10-ounce) packages frozen raspberries in syrup
- 1½ cups sugar
- ½ lemon, sliced
- 1½ cups vodka

Defrost raspberries completely. Drain juice into large saucepan; reserve raspberries.

Combine sugar and lemon slices with raspberry juice.

Microwave cooking method: Stirring often, microwave mixture on high 3 to 5 minutes or until sugar is dissolved and mixture boils. Remove from oven.

Conventional cooking method: Stirring often, cook mixture over low heat until mixture boils. Remove from heat.

Skim any foam from top of mixture and remove lemon slices. Add reserved raspberries and vodka to juice mixture. Fill bottle; cap. Store in refrigerator for one month before serving. Shake bottle every week to mix contents. Before serving, pour contents through a fine strainer. Store in refrigerator after opening.
Yield: 24 ounces

CREAM PUFFS WITH RASPBERRY LIQUEUR SAUCE

Cream Puff Pastry is easy to make. Bake several batches and store in the freezer for gift-giving or for holiday entertaining.

CREAM PUFF PASTRY
- 1 cup water
- 6 tablespoons butter
- ⅛ teaspoon salt
- ⅛ teaspoon sugar
- 1 cup flour
- 4 eggs

In a saucepan, bring water, butter, salt, and sugar to a boil; immediately remove from heat. Stir in flour all at once. Return pan to heat for 30 seconds, stirring constantly. Remove from heat. Beat in eggs, one at a time. Beat until mixture is a smooth paste.

Using a metal spoon, drop mixture by heaping tablespoons onto greased baking sheets (non-stick sheets if possible). Bake in a preheated 350 degree oven for 45 minutes. Remove Cream Puffs from sheets and cool on wire racks. Store in airtight containers or freeze.
Yield: 24 2-inch puffs

RASPBERRY LIQUEUR SAUCE
- 1 (10-ounce) package frozen raspberries in syrup, thawed
- 4 tablespoons currant jelly
- ½ teaspoon lemon juice
- 3 tablespoons Raspberry Liqueur
- 1 tablespoon cornstarch
- 1 tablespoon water

In a small saucepan, heat raspberries. Stir in jelly, lemon juice, and liqueur; bring to a boil. Mix cornstarch with water and add to raspberry mixture. Cook until thickened, stirring constantly.
Yield: 1½ cups

IRISH
SMOOTHIE
AND
CHOCOLATE
CUPS

This Irish Smoothie is chocolaty good, velvety smooth, and lightly laced with coffee. It's so rich and creamy you could eat it with a spoon. And that is what your friends will do if you include with your gift a package of Chocolate Cups for ice cream.

An old-fashioned milk bottle is a perfect container for this creamy concoction, and individual creamers make matching liqueur glasses. A gift to enjoy!

IRISH SMOOTHIE

Our delicious smoothie is especially good in a hot cup of coffee or served over ice cream in a Chocolate Cup.

- ½ cup brandy
- ¾ cup Irish whiskey
- 1 cup sweetened condensed milk
- 2 cups heavy cream
- 2 tablespoons chocolate syrup
- 1 tablespoon instant coffee
- 1 teaspoon vanilla
- 1 teaspoon almond extract

Combine all ingredients in blender; mix well. Fill bottle; cap. Store in refrigerator.
Yield: 34 ounces

CHOCOLATE CUPS

Chocolate cups make perfect containers for chocolate mousse or fresh fruit.

- 4 (1-ounce) squares semisweet chocolate
- 1 tablespoon butter
- 8 fluted foil baking cup liners

In a heavy saucepan, melt chocolate and butter, stirring constantly (watch closely; do not overheat). Cool until slightly thickened. Place 1 tablespoon chocolate in a foil liner; spread over bottom and sides. Place another foil liner on top of chocolate and press lightly. Refrigerate or freeze until firm.

To serve, carefully remove foil liners. Fill with ice cream; top with Irish Smoothie and a fresh sweet cherry.
Yield: 4 chocolate cups

AMARETTO
AND
DOUBLE
CHOCOLATE
CHEESECAKE

Amaretto and cheesecake are an impressive combination. Make that cheesecake chocolate and you have an unforgettable gift that's sure to please even the most discriminating palates.

An ornate bottle filled with Amaretto makes a perfectly lovely gift by itself. But imagine that your gift is a beautifully decorated basket holding the bottle, with a pair of mini chocolate cheesecakes tucked in, too. A sweetly memorable gift, indeed!

AMARETTO

A smooth liqueur; delicious alone, in coffee, or served over ice cream.

- 2 cups sugar
- 1 cup water
- ¾ ounce amaretto extract (available at wine making supply stores)
- 2 cups vodka

In a saucepan, combine sugar and water. Bring to a boil over medium heat and stir for 3 to 4 minutes. Remove from heat. Stir in extract and vodka. Fill bottle; cap. Store in refrigerator for one month before serving. Store in refrigerator after opening.

Yield: approx. 1 quart

DOUBLE CHOCOLATE CHEESECAKE

A creamy filling with a taste of chocolate and Amaretto. You can bake this treat for gifts in six 4½-inch diameter tart pans or in one 9-inch springform pan.

OATMEAL CRUST
- 1 cup quick-cooking oats, uncooked
- ⅓ cup almonds, chopped
- ⅓ cup light brown sugar, firmly packed
- 4 tablespoons butter, softened
- ½ teaspoon cinnamon

In a food processor or blender, combine all ingredients and blend. Press mixture into pan (mixture should be crumbly, but will hold together when pressed into pan). Bake in a preheated 350 degree oven for 6 to 8 minutes. Cool on wire rack.

CHOCOLATE CHEESE FILLING
- 2 (8-ounce) packages cream cheese, softened
- ½ cup sugar
- ¼ cup Amaretto
- 4 eggs
- 4 (1-ounce) squares semisweet chocolate, melted

Beat cheese with sugar and Amaretto. Add eggs, one at a time, beating after each addition. Stir in chocolate, mixing until thick and smooth. Spoon into baked crust. Bake in a preheated 350 degree oven for 30 to 35 minutes or until center is firm. Cool and frost with Chocolate Glaze.

CHOCOLATE GLAZE
- 1 (4-ounce) bar sweet dark chocolate, broken
- 1 tablespoon butter
- 3 tablespoons heavy cream
- ¼ teaspoon Amaretto

In a small saucepan, melt chocolate and butter; stir until smooth. Remove pan from heat; stir in cream and Amaretto. Spread glaze over baked and cooled cheesecake. Chill for several hours before serving.

Yield: one 9-inch cheesecake or six 4½-inch cheesecakes

ZESTY VINEGARS

If you're looking for some zesty ideas for this year's gifts from your kitchen, may we suggest flavored vinegars. Herbed Lemon Vinegar, Blueberry Vinegar, and Garlic Vinegar are all zesty blends of herbs and spices that are sure to spark the imaginations of the cooks on your Christmas list.

These versatile vinegars may be used in anything from soup to dessert — dress a salad, baste the meat, or serve over fresh fruit. We have included some of our favorite recipes for using the vinegars; you may wish to include them with your gift. Present your gift in a decorative bottle and listen for the sparkling comments.

HERBED LEMON VINEGAR

We made our beautiful lemon vinegar with fresh tarragon.

- 4 cups (32 ounces) white wine vinegar
- 4 lemons
- 4 small sprigs fresh dill, basil, or tarragon

Heat vinegar to boiling.

Using paring knife, peel each lemon in a continuous spiral. Place lemon peel and herb sprigs in bottle. Fill bottle; cap. Refrigerate at least two days to blend flavors. Store in refrigerator.

Yield: 32 ounces

WALNUT CITRUS SALAD

Tangy orange and grapefruit sections are combined with fresh, crisp salad greens.

LEMON DRESSING
- ¾ cup vegetable oil
- ¼ cup olive oil
- ¼ cup Herbed Lemon Vinegar
- ½ cup honey
  Juice of 1 lemon

In a small mixing bowl, blend all ingredients with a whisk. Set aside.

Yield: 1¾ cups

SALAD
- 6 cups mixed salad greens such as romaine, bibb, and iceberg
- 1 cup walnut halves
- ¼ cup butter
- 1 medium purple onion, thinly sliced
- 1 cup fresh orange sections, peeled
- 1 cup fresh grapefruit sections, peeled

Wash and dry salad greens. Place in a plastic bag in refrigerator.

Sauté nuts in butter until lightly toasted.

Break salad greens into bite-size pieces and place in a large bowl; add onions. Toss mixture with dressing until coated. Add nuts and fruit; toss again.

Yield: 6 servings

BLUEBERRY VINEGAR

Rice wine vinegar is best to use when making fruit-flavored vinegar. Vinegar should have at least a 5 percent acidity level.

- 2 cups frozen blueberries, thawed
- 4 cups (32 ounces) rice or white wine vinegar

In a saucepan, combine 1 cup berries with vinegar. Heat for 10 minutes, but do not boil. Place remaining berries in bottle. Strain vinegar through a fine strainer. Fill bottle; cap. Store in refrigerator.

Yield: 32 ounces

FRESH FRUIT WITH BLUEBERRY DRESSING
- ½ cup mayonnaise
- 2 teaspoons confectioners' sugar
- ½ cup heavy cream
- 2 tablespoons Blueberry Vinegar
  Fresh fruit such as apples, kiwi, and grapes

In a small bowl, combine mayonnaise, sugar, cream, and vinegar; mix with a whisk until blended. Pour over sliced fruit.

Yield: 1 cup

GARLIC VINEGAR

- 4 cups (32 ounces) red wine vinegar
- 4 garlic cloves, peeled and trimmed to fit in bottle
  Wooden skewer to fit in bottle

Heat vinegar to boiling. Thread garlic cloves on skewer; carefully insert in bottle. Fill bottle; cap. Store in refrigerator.

Yield: 32 ounces

QUICK TURKEY SALAD

GARLIC DRESSING
- 1 clove garlic
- 2 teaspoons sugar
- ½ teaspoon dry mustard
- 4 tablespoons Garlic Vinegar
- ½ teaspoon Worcestershire sauce
  Salt and pepper
- 8 tablespoons vegetable oil

In a small bowl, mash garlic with the back of a spoon. Add sugar and work into a paste. Add mustard, Garlic Vinegar, and Worcestershire. Salt and pepper to taste; whip in the oil. Set aside.

Yield: approx. ¾ cup

SALAD
- 3 cups cooked turkey, chopped
- 3 green onions, chopped, including tops
- ½ cup stuffed green olives, sliced
- ½ cup sliced almonds, toasted
- ½ pound red seedless grapes, sliced

Combine all ingredients in a serving bowl. Add Garlic Dressing and toss. Refrigerate at least one hour before serving.

Yield: 4 to 6 servings

115

GIFT BREADS

Gifts from the kitchen are always appreciated, especially at Christmastime and especially when those gifts are home-baked breads. These three recipes are all quick because they have no yeast and therefore require no rising time. We baked our breads in cans and mini loaf pans to make gift-giving fun and different.

A loaf of Lemon Nut Bread baked in a l-pound coffee can makes an impressive gift. Or you can bake all the breads in small cans and fill your baskets with an assortment. One or two mini loaves in a small market basket make a perfect gift for teacher.

When the recipe yields two standard loaves, you can expect it to make three loaves if using l-pound coffee cans or five to seven loaves if using soup or vegetable cans. Fill the cans two-thirds full and remember this: the smaller the can, the shorter the baking time.

MINCED PUMPKIN BREAD

A spicy, moist bread; excellent sliced and served with whipped cream cheese.

    1   cup vegetable oil
    3   cups sugar
    4   eggs
  2½   cups cooked pumpkin
  1¼   cups mincemeat
  1½   cups pecans, chopped
  3¼   cups flour
    1   teaspoon cinnamon
    1   teaspoon baking powder
  1½   teaspoons salt
  1½   teaspoons nutmeg
    2   teaspoons baking soda

Blend oil and sugar. Add eggs, pumpkin, mincemeat, and nuts.

Combine dry ingredients; stir into sugar mixture until well blended.

Spoon mixture into three greased and floured 9 x 5-inch pans. Bake in a preheated 350 degree oven for 50 minutes or until wooden pick inserted in center comes out clean. Cool in pans for 30 minutes. Freezes well.

Yield: 3 loaves

CRUSTY NUTMEG BREAD

Freshly grated nutmeg gives this butter-flavored bread a true holiday taste.

    3   cups flour, sifted
   ¾   cup butter, softened
  2¼   cups light brown sugar, firmly packed
   ¾   cup pecans, chopped
    2   eggs
    1   teaspoon nutmeg
    1   teaspoon vanilla
    1   cup sour cream
  1½   teaspoons baking soda

For topping: Mix ¼ cup each of flour, butter, sugar, and nuts. Set aside.

Cream remaining butter and sugar, beating until light and fluffy. Add eggs, nutmeg, and vanilla. Beat again.

Combine sour cream and soda in a separate bowl; stir into butter mixture. Add remaining flour and nuts.

Spoon mixture into two greased and floured 9 x 5-inch pans. Sprinkle with reserved topping. Bake in a preheated 350 degree oven for 45 to 50 minutes or until wooden pick inserted in center comes out clean. Cool in pans for 10 minutes. Remove bread from pans and cool on wire racks.

Yield: 2 loaves

(Continued from page 116.)

LEMON NUT BREAD

A delicately textured bread. For an elegant gift, we topped our lemon nut bread with a Citrus Glaze.

    1   cup butter, softened
 1½   cups sugar
    4   eggs, separated (reserve whites)
 3½   tablespoons grated lemon peel
    3   cups cake flour, sifted
 2½   teaspoons baking powder
    1   teaspoon salt
 1½   cups walnuts, finely chopped
    1   cup milk
    1   tablespoon lemon juice
        Citrus Glaze (recipe follows)

Cream butter and sugar, beating until fluffy. Add egg yolks one at a time. Stir in lemon peel.

Combine flour, baking powder, salt, and nuts. Stirring by hand, add flour mixture to butter mixture. Stir in milk and lemon juice.

Beat egg whites until stiff; fold into butter mixture one-half at a time.

Spoon mixture into two greased and floured 9 x 5-inch pans. Bake in a preheated 350 degree oven for 40 to 45 minutes or until wooden pick inserted in center comes out clean. Cool in pans for 10 minutes. Remove bread from pans and cool on wire racks. Glaze if desired.

Yield: 2 loaves

CITRUS GLAZE

 ¼   cup lemon juice
 ¼   cup orange juice
 ¼   cup pineapple juice
   2   tablespoons butter
 2½   cups confectioners' sugar

Heat juices and butter. Stir in sugar; blend until smooth. Spoon glaze over tops of breads, allowing glaze to drizzle down sides.

SAVORY SNACKS

'Tis the season to be baking. But if time is scarce and your gift list is incomplete, packaged breads and crackers can help you create "homemade" snacks.

Savory Breadsticks are rolled in butter and seasonings, then baked for ten minutes. Dilly Oyster Crackers are simply seasoned and require no baking. But, wow, what flavor! We piled the crackers in a tin sleigh, ready for the big ride. A colorful cloth adds a festive touch to the bucket of breadsticks.

SAVORY BREADSTICKS

 ¾   cup butter or margarine
 ½   tablespoon instant beef bouillon
 ⅛   teaspoon marjoram
   1   tablespoon dried parsley
   2   (4½-ounce) packages prepared
        breadsticks
   2   tablespoons Parmesan cheese, grated

Melt butter in a baking sheet. Blend in bouillon and herbs. Roll breadsticks in butter mixture and sprinkle with cheese. Bake in a preheated 300 degree oven for 10 minutes. Store in airtight container until ready to serve.

Yield: 30 breadsticks

DILLY OYSTER CRACKERS

   1   (1.6-ounce) package ranch-style salad
        dressing mix
   1   tablespoon dill weed
 ½   teaspoon garlic powder
   1   (16-ounce) box oyster crackers,
        unseasoned
   1   cup vegetable oil

In a large bowl, combine dressing mix, dill weed, and garlic powder. Add crackers and blend thoroughly. Pour oil over mixture and stir thoroughly; allow crackers to absorb oil and seasonings. Store in airtight container.

Yield: 8 cups

SWEET TREATS

Colorful, decorative tins filled with tasty homemade treats are a wonderful way to say ''Have a very merry Christmas.''

A slab of creamy, dreamy Peanut Butter Fudge tied with a satin ribbon makes a great gift, or you can cut the fudge in simple shapes and decorate each piece with chocolate and nuts. The Chocolate Apricot Roll is really quick and easy, to be so delicious. Fresh orange and toasted pecans make the Orange Creams especially good. Potato chips dipped in chocolate are a tasty combination of sweet and salty.

With four recipes to choose from, these two pages should answer lots of your what-to-give-to-who questions.

PEANUT BUTTER FUDGE

```
1   cup sugar
1   cup light brown sugar, firmly packed
1   cup evaporated milk
4   tablespoons light corn syrup
    Pinch of salt
1   cup large marshmallows, cut in pieces
½   cup peanut butter
2   tablespoons butter
1   teaspoon vanilla
```

In a medium saucepan, cook sugars, milk, syrup, and salt to the soft-ball stage (240 degrees on a candy thermometer). Just before removing from heat, add marshmallows, peanut butter, and butter. Stir until blended and set aside to cool. Add vanilla and beat; pour into a buttered 8 x 8-inch pan. Cool completely. Store in airtight container or see Chocolate Dipped Variation (recipe follows).
Yield: one 8-inch square

CHOCOLATE DIPPED VARIATION

Dipping chocolate is called chocolate bark in the supermarket. For the chocolate-loving purist, ask at a kitchen specialty shop for chocolate summer coating or commercial coating chocolate.

```
6   ounces dark dipping chocolate, melted
¾   cup pecans, finely ground
```
Cut cooled Peanut Butter Fudge into various shapes. Dip edges into chocolate, then into nuts. Place on waxed paper to dry. Store in airtight container.

ORANGE CREAMS

A smooth candy with the taste of fresh orange and toasted pecans.

```
2    cups sugar
4    tablespoons light corn syrup
¾    cup milk
⅛    teaspoon salt
1    medium orange, juiced and the rind grated
4    tablespoons butter
1    teaspoon vanilla
1½   cups pecans, lightly toasted and chopped
```

In a heavy saucepan, combine sugar, syrup, milk, and salt. Bring to a boil. Add orange juice. Lower heat and cook until soft-ball stage (240 degrees on a candy thermometer). Test by dropping one-half teaspoon candy in a cup of cold water. A soft ball will form when candy is ready.

Add grated rind and cook one minute more. Remove from heat. Blend in butter and vanilla and set aside to cool.

Beat until candy begins to lose its shine. Test a few drops of candy on a plate. When it holds its shape, add nuts. Drop by teaspoonfuls onto waxed paper. Store in airtight container.
Yield: 32 to 36 pieces

CHOCOLATE APRICOT ROLL

A no-fuss candy for your chocolate-loving friends.

```
16   large marshmallows, cut into pieces
2    tablespoons milk
4    ounces dark dipping chocolate, melted
1    cup pecans, finely chopped
1    cup dried apricots, chopped
```

In a double boiler, melt marshmallows in milk. Stir until smooth. Add chocolate, nuts, and apricots.

Form into a 12-inch roll. Place in refrigerator until firm; slice.
Yield: one 12-inch roll

CHOCOLATE CHIPS

So easy, good, and elegant! These chips are best if eaten or shared with friends soon after preparing.

```
24   perfect ridge-style potato chips
6    ounces dark dipping chocolate
```

Melt chocolate according to package directions. Remove from heat.

Carefully dip one half of each potato chip in chocolate. Place on waxed paper or foil. Let chocolate dry completely before storing in an airtight container.
Yield: 24 chips

THE TASTES OF CHRISTMAS

The tantalizing tastes of Christmas bring us an abundance of pleasures.
Good food and holiday cheer are always at the heart of the celebration when
friends and relatives gather. To help you treat your guests to Christmas
at its best, we bring you plans and recipes for four delightful
parties. All the recipes have been developed in our own Test
Kitchen, so you can be assured of delicious, eye-appealing foods.
When you open your home to friends and neighbors, our Holiday Open
House will satisfy their appetites with sumptuous foods for casual dining.
On Christmas Day, your loved ones will enjoy our Festive Family Dinner,
which offers an enticing twist to the traditional turkey dinner. And of
course it isn't Christmas without cookies, so we've planned a party
just for trading treats. We've included 21 cookie recipes to help you
choose just the right one to contribute to your Christmas Cookie Klatch.
You'll also want to set aside a special day during the yuletide
to wake up your taste buds with a Merry Country Brunch.
Make plans now to share the Christmas spirit in a delicious way!

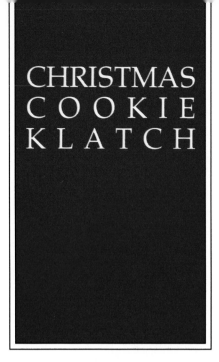

CHRISTMAS COOKIE KLATCH

Here's a sweet idea for a party with your dearest friends: a Christmas Cookie Klatch where treats are traded and enjoyed. Each guest is asked to bring a batch of one kind of cookie, and everyone gets to choose an assortment to take home. So that the nibbling doesn't deplete everyone's assortment, plan to serve a few extra batches of cookies with our Wassail Punch.

Lemon Bars

Date Bars

Cream Cheese Spritz

Cinnamon Bars

Almond Crisps

Fruitcake Christmas Cookies

Shortbread

Caramel Graham Crackers

Meringue Delights

White Chocolate Chunk Macadamia Cookies

Wreath Cookies

Cheesecake Bites

Filbert Cookies

Clove Cookies

Eggnog Cookies

Sugar Cookies

Cream Cheese Preserve Cookies

Chocolate Gingerbread

Mexican Chocolate Cookies

Triple Chip Cookies

Mint Patties

Wassail Punch

CHRISTMAS COOKIE KLATCH

WASSAIL PUNCH

    1 quart boiling water
    4 spiced tea bags
    1 gallon apple cider
    2 quarts orange juice
    1 quart cranberry juice
 1½ cups sugar
    1 whole orange
   12 whole cloves
    4 cinnamon sticks
  ½ cup small red cinnamon candies

Pour water over tea bags and steep for 4 minutes; remove tea bags.

In large pot, combine tea, apple cider, orange juice, cranberry juice, and sugar. Bring to a boil and reduce heat to simmer.

Stud whole orange with cloves. Add orange, cinnamon sticks, and cinnamon candies to punch. Simmer for 30 minutes; serve hot.

Yield: 2 gallons

TRIPLE CHIP COOKIES

    1 cup butter or margarine, softened
 1½ cups light brown sugar, firmly packed
  ½ cup sugar
    2 eggs
    2 teaspoons vanilla
    2 cups flour
    1 teaspoon baking soda
  ½ teaspoon baking powder
  ½ teaspoon salt
 1½ cups semisweet chocolate chips
    1 cup peanut butter chips
  ¾ cup butterscotch chips

Cream butter and sugars. Beat in eggs and vanilla.

Combine flour, baking soda, baking powder, and salt; gradually add to creamed mixture. Stir in chips.

Drop by heaping teaspoonfuls onto greased baking sheets. Bake in a preheated 350 degree oven for 10 to 12 minutes or just until done. Do not overbake.

Yield: approx. 6 dozen cookies

CARAMEL GRAHAM CRACKERS

Our nickname for this cookie is ''Tastes Better Than It Looks Cookie.''

   24 2½-inch cinnamon graham cracker
        squares
  ½ cup margarine
  ½ cup butter
    1 cup light brown sugar, firmly packed
    1 cup pecans, chopped

Line a 15½ x 10½ x 1-inch baking sheet with foil; cover with single layer of graham crackers.

Mix margarine, butter, and sugar in a saucepan; bring to a boil and cook for 2 minutes.

Pour mixture over crackers; sprinkle nuts on top. Bake in a preheated 350 degree oven for 12 minutes. Cut into triangles while warm.

Yield: approx. 4 dozen cookies

CLOVE COOKIES

  ½ cup butter or margarine, melted
    1 cup sugar
    1 teaspoon vanilla
    1 egg
    1 cup flour
    1 teaspoon ground cloves

Stir butter and sugar together; add vanilla. Beat in egg until mixture is smooth.

Stir flour and cloves together; blend with butter mixture.

Drop by teaspoonfuls, 2 inches apart, onto lightly greased baking sheets. Bake in a preheated 350 degree oven for 8 to 10 minutes or until lightly browned. Cool slightly before removing from baking sheets.

Yield: approx. 4 dozen cookies

CREAM CHEESE PRESERVE COOKIES

    1 (8-ounce) package cream cheese,
        softened
    1 cup unsalted butter, softened
    2 cups flour
        Grated rind of ½ lemon or dash of
        lemon juice
        Blackberry, apricot, and strawberry
        preserves

Beat cream cheese and butter together until well blended. Add flour and lemon; mix well. Form into four balls of equal size; wrap in waxed paper and refrigerate until firm.

Roll out one ball at a time between two sheets of waxed paper to ¼-inch thickness. Cut out with 2½-inch round scalloped-edge cookie cutter.

Place cookies on ungreased baking sheets. On one side of cookie, place a 1-inch wide heart cookie cutter ¼ inch from the edge; cut out heart (refer to photo, page 124). Place a small amount of preserves on the other side of cookie. Fold cookie in half and press edges together.

Bake in a preheated 375 degree oven for 15 to 20 minutes or until slightly puffed and just beginning to brown. Cool slightly before removing from baking sheets.

Yield: approx. 4 dozen cookies

DATE BARS

    1 cup butter or margarine, softened
 2⅓ cups dark brown sugar, firmly packed
    3 eggs
 1½ teaspoons vanilla
    3 cups flour
    1 teaspoon baking powder
  ½ teaspoon baking soda
    3 cups pitted dates, coarsely chopped
    1 cup pecans, chopped

Cream butter and sugar until light and fluffy. Beat in eggs, one at a time. Stir in vanilla.

Combine flour, baking powder, and baking soda; gradually add to creamed mixture. Stir in dates and nuts. Spread batter in a greased 13 x 9 x 2-inch baking pan. Bake in a preheated 375 degree oven for 25 minutes. Cool in pan and cut into bars.

Yield: approx. 2 dozen bars

These rich cookies offer old-fashioned goodness, especially when you serve them in quaint baskets, wooden bowls and trays, and napkin-lined grapevine wreaths: *(clockwise from top right)* Caramel Graham Crackers, Date Bars, Cream Cheese Preserve Cookies, Triple Chip Cookies, and Clove Cookies.

WHITE CHOCOLATE CHUNK MACADAMIA COOKIES

1 cup butter or margarine, softened
1 cup light brown sugar, firmly packed
½ cup sugar
2 eggs
1 teaspoon vanilla
2¼ cups flour
1 teaspoon baking soda
1 teaspoon salt
1 cup macadamia nuts, coarsely chopped
2 cups white chocolate (or almond bark), broken into bite-sized chunks

Cream butter and sugars until light and fluffy. Beat in eggs and vanilla.
Combine flour, soda, and salt; gradually add to creamed mixture. Stir in nuts and chocolate.
Drop by heaping teaspoonfuls onto greased baking sheets. Bake in a preheated 350 degree oven for 10 to 12 minutes. Cool slightly before removing from baking sheets.
Yield: approx. 6 dozen cookies

CINNAMON BARS

1 cup butter or margarine, softened
¾ cup sugar
2 cups flour, sifted
3 teaspoons cinnamon
1 egg, separated
1 teaspoon vanilla
1 cup pecans, chopped

Cream butter and sugar. Combine flour and cinnamon; gradually add to creamed mixture. Stir in egg yolk and vanilla until well blended.
Spread dough in a greased 15½ x 10½ x 1-inch baking sheet and pat down. Brush egg white on top of dough; sprinkle nuts over dough. Press nuts into dough.
Bake in a preheated 300 degree oven for 30 minutes. Cut into bars and remove from sheet to cool.
Yield: approx. 2 dozen bars

EGGNOG COOKIES

For a country touch, we decorated some of these cookies with nutmeg. Place the center section of a paper doily on cookie and sprinkle with ground nutmeg.

1 cup butter or margarine, softened
2 cups sugar
1 teaspoon vanilla
4 eggs
3 cups flour
2 teaspoons baking powder
½ teaspoon nutmeg
½ teaspoon salt

Cream butter, sugar, and vanilla. Beat in eggs, one at a time. Sift dry ingredients together; gradually add to creamed mixture. Cover and refrigerate several hours.
Drop by heaping teaspoonfuls onto ungreased baking sheets. Bake in a preheated 375 degree oven for 6 to 8 minutes or until lightly browned around the edges. Cool slightly before removing from baking sheets.
Yield: approx. 8 dozen cookies

CHOCOLATE GINGERBREAD

Our gingerbread teddy bear is shown with a festive bow around his neck. If desired, you may decorate with frosting.

½ cup butter or margarine, softened
¾ cup dark brown sugar, firmly packed
½ cup dark corn syrup
¼ cup molasses
1 egg
3 cups flour
½ cup cocoa
1 teaspoon ginger
1 teaspoon ground cloves
Buttercream Frosting (recipe on this page)

Cream butter, sugar, corn syrup, and molasses. Add egg and beat until well blended. Add flour, cocoa, and spices; stir until blended, adding more flour if necessary to make a stiff dough. Chill at least 1 hour.
Roll out dough on a floured surface to ⅛-inch thickness. Cut out with desired cookie cutters and place on ungreased baking sheets. Bake in a preheated 325 degree oven for 8 to 12 minutes. Cool and remove from baking sheets.
Yield: approx. 3 dozen cookies

FRUITCAKE CHRISTMAS COOKIES

½ cup butter or margarine, softened
1 cup sugar
1 egg, beaten
½ teaspoon baking soda
¼ cup sour milk
1¾ to 2 cups flour
½ teaspoon salt
¾ cup candied cherries, chopped
¾ cup dates, chopped
¾ cup pecans, chopped
Buttercream Frosting (recipe follows)
Red and green candied cherries

Cream butter and sugar; add egg. Stir together baking soda and sour milk; gradually add to creamed mixture. (**Note:** Milk may be soured by stirring 1 tablespoon lemon juice or vinegar into scant ¼ cup whole milk.)
Combine flour and salt; gradually add to creamed mixture. Stir in fruit and nuts until well blended.
Drop by teaspoonfuls onto greased baking sheets. Bake in a preheated 350 degree oven for 10 to 12 minutes. Cool on wire racks.
Decorate with Buttercream Frosting and red and green cherries.
Yield: approx. 3 dozen cookies

BUTTERCREAM FROSTING

2 cups confectioners' sugar
2 tablespoons butter or margarine
1 tablespoon milk
1 teaspoon vanilla
Blend all ingredients until smooth. Add more milk or sugar as necessary to achieve spreading consistency.

SHORTBREAD

For our shortbread, we used a stoneware mold designed especially for cookie baking. However, shortbread can also be patted into circles and then cut into wedges or cut out with cookie cutters. The best thing about old-fashioned shortbread is that it can be made several days in advance and it gets better with age.

1 cup butter, softened
½ cup sugar
2½ cups flour, sifted

Cream butter; gradually add sugar and blend until light and fluffy. Stir in flour until well blended. Cover with waxed paper and chill for several hours.
Work with half of dough at a time and store remainder in refrigerator. Roll dough out on floured surface to ½-inch thickness; cut out with desired cookie cutters. Place on ungreased baking sheets. Bake in a preheated 300 degree oven for 30 minutes. Cool slightly before removing from sheets.
Yield: approx. 3½ dozen cookies

Here's a collection of cookies to please your country-lovin' heart: *(clockwise from top right)* Eggnog Cookies, Cinnamon Bars, Chocolate Gingerbread, Shortbread, Fruitcake Christmas Cookies, and White Chocolate Chunk Macadamia Cookies.

CHRISTMAS COOKIE KLATCH

HELPFUL HINTS

To ensure even baking, use baking sheets with low sides and place one baking sheet at a time in the center of the oven to allow proper circulation.

To shorten your time in the kitchen, line baking sheets with foil. You can have an extra sheet of foil covered with cookies and ready to slide onto the baking sheet and pop in the oven.

Overworking cookie dough will cause toughness.

SUGAR COOKIES

Our sugar cookies are decorated with colorful frosting made using the Butter Frosting recipe. To give the glazed angels the look of beautiful porcelain, we frosted them with the Pastel Glaze (recipe on page 131; omit red food coloring), and let them dry overnight.

    ½   cup butter, softened
    ½   cup shortening
    1   cup sugar
    1½ teaspoons vanilla
    3   eggs
    3½ cups flour
    2   teaspoons cream of tartar
    1   teaspoon baking soda
        Butter Frosting (recipe follows)

Cream butter, shortening, sugar, and vanilla until light and fluffy. Add eggs, one at a time, beating well after each addition.
Combine flour, cream of tartar, and soda; gradually add to creamed mixture. Cover and refrigerate several hours.
Work with half of the dough at a time and store remainder in refrigerator. Roll dough out on lightly floured surface to ¼-inch thickness; cut out with desired cookie cutters.
Place on lightly greased baking sheets. Bake in a preheated 425 degree oven for 6 to 8 minutes or until lightly browned. Store in airtight containers, placing waxed paper between layers of cookies.
Yield: approx. 5½ dozen cookies

BUTTER FROSTING
    3   cups confectioners' sugar, sifted
    ¼   cup butter, melted and cooled
    ¼   cup cream or milk
    ½   teaspoon vanilla
        Food coloring
Blend sugar and butter. Add cream and vanilla; beat until smooth. Tint mixture with food coloring and decorate cookies.

These festive cookies say Christmas in a merry way: *(clockwise from top)* Lemon Bars, Wreath Cookies, Sugar Cookies decorated with Butter Frosting or Pastel Glaze, Cheesecake Bites, and Mexican Chocolate Cookies.

LEMON BARS

    2   cups flour
    ½   cup confectioners' sugar
    1   cup butter or margarine, melted
    4   eggs, slightly beaten
    2   cups sugar
    ¼   cup flour
    1   teaspoon baking powder
    ¼   cup lemon juice
    2   cups coconut

Combine flour and confectioners' sugar. Add melted butter; mix well. Spread mixture in a greased 13 x 9 x 2-inch baking pan. Bake in a preheated 350 degree oven for 20 to 25 minutes.
Stir eggs and sugar together. Combine flour and baking powder; add to sugar mixture. Stir in lemon juice and coconut. Pour over baked crust. Return to oven and bake for 30 minutes. Cool and glaze.

GLAZE
    1¾ cups confectioners' sugar
    3   to 4 tablespoons lemon juice
Blend sugar and lemon juice together; pour over baked mixture. Cut into bars.
Yield: approx. 2 dozen bars

CHEESECAKE BITES

    ⅓   cup light brown sugar, firmly packed
    1   cup flour
    ½   cup pecans, chopped
    ⅓   cup butter or margarine, melted
    1   (8-ounce) package cream cheese, softened
    ¼   cup sugar
    1   egg
    2   tablespoons milk
    1   tablespoon lemon juice
    1   teaspoon vanilla

Mix brown sugar, flour, and nuts. Stir in butter until blended. Reserve ⅓ cup of mixture; pat remainder in a greased 8-inch square baking pan. Bake in a preheated 350 degree oven for 12 to 15 minutes.
Beat cream cheese and sugar until smooth. Beat in remaining ingredients. Pour over baked crust; sprinkle with reserved pecan mixture. Return to oven and bake for 25 minutes. Cool slightly; then cut into 2-inch squares.
Yield: approx. 16 squares

MEXICAN CHOCOLATE COOKIES

These special cookies can also decorate your Christmas tree, hang on a wreath, or dress up a kitchen window. If you plan to hang the cookie, make a hole in the top with a toothpick before baking.

    1½ cups butter, softened
    1¾ cups sugar
    2   eggs, slightly beaten
    3   cups flour
    1½ cups cocoa
    ¼   teaspoon salt
    ½   teaspoon black pepper
    1   teaspoon cinnamon
    4   to 6 ounces semisweet chocolate, melted

Cream butter and sugar; add eggs and beat until fluffy.
Sift dry ingredients together; gradually add to creamed mixture. Beat until well blended, adding more flour if dough seems too soft.
Divide dough into thirds and wrap in plastic wrap; chill at least 1 hour.
On floured board, roll out dough to ⅛-inch thickness; cut out with desired cookie cutters. Place on greased baking sheets. Bake in a preheated 375 degree oven for 8 to 10 minutes or until crisp but not darkened. Cool on wire racks; then drizzle melted chocolate on cookie tops.
Yield: approx. 3 dozen cookies

WREATH COOKIES

    3   tablespoons butter or margarine
    ½   cup light corn syrup
    ¾   teaspoon green food coloring
    3   tablespoons sugar
    3½ cups cornflake cereal
        Small red cinnamon candies

In a large saucepan, mix butter, corn syrup, food coloring, and sugar. Cook over medium heat until mixture boils, stirring constantly. Boil for 5 minutes, stirring frequently; remove from heat. Add cereal and stir until well blended.
Drop mixture by buttered ¼ cup measure onto waxed paper. With buttered fingers, shape each portion to resemble a wreath; decorate with cinnamon candies. Let stand until firm. Store in airtight containers.
Yield: approx. 12 wreaths

CHRISTMAS COOKIE KLATCH

HELPFUL HINTS

Store cookies in airtight containers. Delicate cookies should be wrapped individually for protection from breakage.

When thawing frozen baked cookies, leave wrapped or in containers to prevent them from drying out.

Use popcorn as a filler when packing cookies for mailing.

ALMOND CRISPS

The secret to this recipe is to form cookies quickly after removing baking sheet from oven.

- ⅔ cup plus 2 tablespoons blanched almonds, finely ground
- ½ cup sugar
- ½ cup butter or margarine
- 1 tablespoon flour
- 2 tablespoons cream

Combine all ingredients in a 10-inch skillet. Cook over low heat, stirring constantly, until butter is melted and mixture is blended. Keep skillet warm over very low heat.

Drop mixture by heaping teaspoonfuls, 2 inches apart, onto greased baking sheet. (**Note:** Bake only 4 cookies at a time.) Bake in a preheated 350 degree oven for 5 minutes or until golden.

Use a spatula to loosen and turn cookies over; then quickly roll each one around the handle of a wooden spoon. If cookies get too firm to roll, reheat in oven a minute to soften. Cool rolled cookies on wire racks.

Repeat until all batter is used, greasing baking sheet each time. Store cookies in an airtight container.

Yield: approx. 2½ dozen cookies

MERINGUE DELIGHTS

- 1 egg white
- ¾ cup dark brown sugar, firmly packed
- 1 tablespoon flour
  Pinch of salt
- 1 cup pecans, chopped

Beat egg white until stiff. Add sugar and beat until blended. Stir in flour, salt, and nuts.

Drop by teaspoonfuls, 2 inches apart, onto greased baking sheets. Bake in a preheated 325 degree oven for 10 minutes. Cool slightly before removing from baking sheets.

Yield: approx. 3 dozen cookies

FILBERT COOKIES

We added an elegant Pastel Glaze to some of our filbert cookies. They complement the cookies that were rolled in confectioners' sugar.

- 1 cup butter, softened
- 1 cup sugar
- 2 cups flour
- ¼ teaspoon salt
- 2 teaspoons vanilla
- 1 cup filberts, finely ground
  Confectioners' sugar
  Pastel Glaze (recipe follows)

Use blender or food processor to grind filberts.

Cream butter and sugar; stir in flour, salt, and vanilla. Add nuts and mix well.

Form cookies by rolling teaspoonfuls of dough into balls. Place balls, 1 inch apart, on ungreased baking sheets; flatten slightly. Bake in a preheated 300 degree oven for 18 to 20 minutes. Cool slightly, then roll in confectioners' sugar. Cookies may also be iced with Pastel Glaze.

Yield: approx. 6 dozen cookies

PASTEL GLAZE

The flavor of our glaze can be changed by substituting orange or lemon juice for the water.

- 2½ cups confectioners' sugar, sifted
- 3 to 4 tablespoons hot water
  Red food coloring

Add water and food coloring gradually to sugar. (**Note:** Be careful to add only a few drops of color at a time.) Beat mixture until smooth; drizzle or pour over cookies.

CREAM CHEESE SPRITZ

We decorated this delicate cookie with silver candy dragées. We also dusted the Christmas trees with confectioners' sugar.

- 1 cup shortening
- 1 (3-ounce) package cream cheese, softened
- 1 cup sugar
- 1 egg yolk
- 1 teaspoon vanilla
- 2½ cups flour, sifted
- ½ teaspoon salt
- ¼ teaspoon cinnamon
  Food coloring, if desired

Cream shortening and cheese. Gradually add sugar and mix well. Beat in egg yolk and vanilla.

Sift flour with salt and cinnamon; gradually add to creamed mixture. Tint with food coloring, if desired.

Fill cookie press and form cookies on ungreased baking sheets. Bake in a preheated 350 degree oven for 12 to 15 minutes. Cool before removing from baking sheets.

Yield: approx. 6 dozen cookies

MINT PATTIES

- ½ cup butter, melted
- 1 egg
- 1 cup sugar
- 1¾ cups flour
- 1 teaspoon baking soda
- 1 teaspoon peppermint extract
- 2 cups semisweet chocolate chips
- ¼ bar paraffin

Beat butter, egg, and sugar together.

Combine flour and baking soda; add to butter mixture. Stir in peppermint extract.

Drop by teaspoonfuls onto greased baking sheets. Bake in a preheated 350 degree oven for 10 to 12 minutes. Remove from baking sheets and cool on wire racks.

In double boiler over hot (not boiling) water, melt chips and paraffin. Drop cookies into chocolate to coat. Lift out with a fork and place on wire racks to harden.

Yield: approx. 3 dozen cookies

You'll want to bring out your best silver and crystal serving pieces for these elegant cookies: *(clockwise from top right)* Filbert Cookies, Meringue Delights, Cream Cheese Spritz, Almond Crisps, and Mint Patties.

A
FESTIVE
FAMILY
DINNER

Our Festive Family Dinner recipes bring color and exciting new tastes to the traditional turkey dinner. Twin turkeys offer a bounty of white meat and drumsticks, and a moist cornbread dressing with a hint of herbs enhances the flavorful meat. There's a spicy soup, a tart frozen salad, and lots of festive, fruity vegetables. The crowning touch is an elegant layered dessert that's easy to make. This year, start a new tradition with these delicious versions of your family's favorite Christmas foods. They'll love you for it! This menu serves eight.

Cream of Pumpkin Soup

Rolled Herb Toast

Frosty Cranberry Tiptops

Twin Herb Turkeys

Cornbread Dressing

Gravy

Baked Pineapple Oranges

Almond Broccoli Ring

Holiday Rice

Glazed Baked Onions

Ambrosia Sweet Potatoes

Rolls

English Trifle

A FESTIVE FAMILY DINNER

HELPFUL HINTS

Cream of Pumpkin Soup *may be prepared to the point of adding cream to the cooked mixture, then frozen in a covered container. Before serving, thaw soup and heat slowly; stir in cream and continue heating soup.*

Our **Almond Broccoli Ring** *is an elegant and convenient vegetable for your Christmas dinner. To make ahead, fill baking pan and freeze before baking. There is no need to thaw it, just increase the baking time about 30 minutes.*

CREAM OF PUMPKIN SOUP

  1 onion, thinly sliced
  2 tablespoons butter
  2 cups orange juice
  2 cups cooked pumpkin, mashed
  2 cups chicken broth
  ½ teaspoon mace
  ½ teaspoon salt
  ¼ teaspoon white pepper
  ¼ teaspoon nutmeg
  1 cup light cream

In a large saucepan, sauté the onion in butter until soft. Add orange juice, pumpkin, broth, and seasonings. Simmer for 20 minutes. Puree mixture in a food processor or blender until smooth. Return to saucepan and stir in cream. Heat, being careful not to boil.
Serve immediately. Garnish with a swirl of cream and toasted walnut halves. Sage leaves also add a pretty touch.
Yield: 8 servings

ROLLED HERB TOAST

  ½ cup butter
  1 (½-ounce) package herb salad
      dressing mix
  1 teaspoon dill weed
  ¼ teaspoon garlic salt
  20 slices thin bread

Melt butter in a large baking sheet. Add dry seasonings and mix.
Trim crusts off bread; flatten each slice with a rolling pin and roll tightly. Coat each roll with butter mixture. Bake in a preheated 300 degree oven until lightly browned. Turn several times while baking. Serve hot.
Toast may be frozen or stored in an airtight container. Reheat before serving.
Yield: 20 servings

FROSTY CRANBERRY TIPTOPS

A beautiful layered salad made in advance and frozen in convenient throwaway paper cups.

  1 (16-ounce) can jellied cranberry sauce
  1 (8-ounce) can crushed pineapple,
      drained
  3 tablespoons lemon juice
  1 cup heavy cream
  1 (3-ounce) package cream cheese,
      softened
  ⅓ cup mayonnaise
  ½ cup confectioners' sugar, sifted
  1 cup pecans or walnuts, chopped

Crush cranberry sauce with a fork. Add pineapple and lemon juice; mix thoroughly. Set aside.
Whip cream and mix with cheese, mayonnaise, sugar, and nuts.
Beginning with cranberry mixture, alternate layers of cranberry and cream mixtures in eight 5-ounce paper cups. Freeze until firm. When ready to serve, tear away paper cups and invert on serving plates.
Garnish with fresh salad greens and dollops of whipped cream.
Yield: 8 servings

ALMOND BROCCOLI RING

You will be proud to serve this beautiful vegetable ring on Christmas Day. The broccoli mixture may also be baked in individual custard cups.

  1 (10-ounce) package chopped broccoli
  1 (10-ounce) package broccoli spears
      Salt
  3 tablespoons margarine
  ½ cup green onions, minced, including
      tops
  3 tablespoons flour
  ¼ cup chicken broth
  1 cup sour cream
  3 eggs, lightly beaten
  ¾ cup Swiss cheese, grated
  ½ cup slivered almonds, toasted
  1 teaspoon salt
  ½ teaspoon pepper
  ¾ teaspoon nutmeg, freshly grated
  1 pint cherry tomatoes
  2 tablespoons margarine

Steam broccoli until tender; lightly salt and drain. Using a sharp knife, chop broccoli finely and set aside.
For cream sauce: In a saucepan, melt 3 tablespoons margarine; add onions and sauté lightly. Remove from heat; blend in flour and return to heat. Stirring slowly, cook over medium heat for 2 minutes. Remove from heat; add broth and stir. Return to heat and continue to stir as sauce thickens. Lower heat and cook 2 minutes more. Blend in sour cream and heat thoroughly.
Stir a few tablespoons of sauce into beaten eggs; add egg mixture to remainder of sauce in pan and cook 1 minute, stirring constantly. Blend in cheese. Add broccoli, almonds, and seasonings.
Spoon mixture into an oiled 1-quart ring mold or eight 5-ounce custard cups. Place in a large baking pan that is half filled with hot water. Bake in a preheated 350 degree oven, about 50 minutes for mold (30 minutes for custard cups). The mixture is done when a knife inserted in the center comes out clean. When ready to serve, invert on a serving plate.
Sauté cherry tomatoes in margarine (about 5 to 6 minutes). Garnish with tomatoes and fresh herbs or parsley.
Yield: 8 to 10 servings

(Top left) Our spicy Cream of Pumpkin Soup is served with Rolled Herb Toast.

(Top right) Frosty Cranberry Tiptops combine creamy sweetness with the tartness of the cranberry-pineapple layers.

(Bottom) Sautéed cherry tomatoes add a festive touch to this Almond Broccoli Ring, which features a delicate blend of flavors.

136

A FESTIVE FAMILY DINNER

HELPFUL HINTS

Turkey baking has never been easier for the busy homemaker. Our **Twin Herb Turkeys** are prepared and seasoned the night before baking. The next morning, just remove from the refrigerator and pop in the oven to bake.

To ease last minute cooking time, start **Holiday Rice** early in the day. Brown the rice and cook for 15 minutes. Cover and set aside. Before serving, reheat rice and stir in remaining ingredients.

When you buy a holiday turkey you should plan on ¾ to 1 pound of turkey per person.

GLAZED BAKED ONIONS

This is a good do-ahead recipe. After preparing, cover with foil and refrigerate. Bring to room temperature before drizzling with butter and broiling.

- 4 medium onions
  Chicken broth
- 2 (10-ounce) packages frozen green peas, cooked
- ½ cup soft bread crumbs
- ¼ cup Parmesan cheese, grated
- 2 tablespoons parsley, chopped
- ½ teaspoon dry mustard
- 5 tablespoons butter or margarine
  Melted butter or margarine for glaze

Peel and halve onions. Place in saucepan in 2 inches of chicken broth. Bring to a boil, cover, and lower heat. Let simmer for 20 minutes or until tender but firm. Drain well.

Gently lift out center of onions, leaving a shell 2 to 3 rings thick. Fill centers with peas.

Mix bread crumbs with cheese, parsley, mustard, and butter. Sprinkle over onions; then drizzle with butter. Broil 5 to 7 minutes or until lightly browned. Garnish with pimiento strips.

Yield: 8 servings

(Top) Elegant, individual portions make these Glazed Baked Onions and Baked Pineapple Oranges irresistible.

(Bottom) Ambrosia Sweet Potatoes bring delightful color and zest to the meal.

BAKED PINEAPPLE ORANGES

This tart orange cup may be prepared ahead and requires no refrigeration. We garnished the scalloped edges of the oranges with finely minced parsley.

- 6 large navel oranges
- 4 cups crushed pineapple with juice
  Juice of 1 lemon
- ½ cup sugar
- ¼ cup light brown sugar, firmly packed
- ¼ cup sherry
- ½ teaspoon nutmeg
- ½ cup walnuts, finely chopped

Cut oranges in half and scoop out pulp; reserve orange shells and pulp.

In a saucepan, combine pulp, pineapple, lemon juice, and sugars. Cook slowly until thickened, stirring often. Add sherry and nutmeg to thickened mixture.

While pineapple mixture cooks, scallop edges of orange shells. Spoon mixture into shells and sprinkle with nuts. Bake in a preheated 350 degree oven for 20 minutes. Serve at room temperature.

Yield: 12 servings

HOLIDAY RICE

- 1¼ cups long-grain rice, uncooked
- 2 tablespoons butter
- 2 cups chicken broth
- ½ cup water
- ½ teaspoon salt
- ½ teaspoon pepper
- ¾ teaspoon sage
- 1½ teaspoons sugar
- 1 small red apple, cored and chopped
- 1 small green apple, cored and chopped
- 2 celery ribs, thinly sliced
- ¾ cup carrots, thinly sliced
- ¼ cup golden raisins
- ⅓ cup light cream
- ⅓ cup sliced almonds

In a heavy skillet, lightly brown rice in butter. Add broth, water, salt, pepper, sage, and sugar. Bring to a boil; cover, reduce heat, and simmer 15 minutes. Add remaining ingredients and cook for 3 minutes.

Yield: 6 to 8 servings

AMBROSIA SWEET POTATOES

- 6 cups sliced sweet potatoes, cooked
- 1 orange, sliced
- 1 cup crushed pineapple with juice
- ½ cup light brown sugar, firmly packed
- ½ cup butter, melted
- ½ teaspoon salt
- ½ cup shredded coconut

In a buttered 2-quart casserole, alternate layers of potatoes and orange slices.

Mix pineapple, sugar, butter, and salt. Pour mixture over layers. Sprinkle coconut on top.

Bake in a preheated 350 degree oven for 30 minutes.

Yield: 8 to 10 servings

TWIN HERB TURKEYS

Our turkey platter is garnished with steamed fresh miniature corn and beets. We added some fresh herbs for a picture perfect holiday dinner.

- 4 onions
- 2 green peppers
- 8 garlic cloves
- 1 cup parsley
- 2 teaspoons pepper
- 1 cup butter
- 2 turkeys, 9 to 10 pounds each
- 2 teaspoons salt

In a food processor or blender, puree onion, green pepper, garlic, parsley, and pepper. Sauté mixture in butter until vegetables are soft and mixture forms a paste.

Rub turkeys with salt. Pierce skin of turkeys and coat with the herb paste. Cover and refrigerate overnight.

Preheat oven to 325 degrees. Place meat thermometer in one turkey thigh, but do not touch the bone. Roast breast side down 15 to 20 minutes per pound or until thermometer reaches 185 degrees. Turn breast side up and brown (10 to 15 minutes). Cool before slicing.

Yield: 14 to 16 servings

A
FESTIVE
FAMILY
DINNER

HELPFUL HINTS

Our **Cornbread Dressing** *is a traditional Southern recipe. It is moist and lightly seasoned. Make cornbread several days ahead and freeze. The dressing should have a fluffy texture before baking.*

To properly thaw frozen turkey, leave turkey in the original wrapper and thaw in the refrigerator 24 hours per 5 pounds of turkey. To rush thawing, cover with cold water. Allow ½ hour per pound, changing the water often. Once thawed, either cook or refrigerate immediately.

GRAVY

      Neck and giblets from one turkey
  4   to 5 cups water
  2   celery ribs
  1   small onion, halved
  1   bay leaf
      Salt and pepper
  4   tablespoons butter, divided
  3   tablespoons flour
  ½   cup onion, chopped
  ¼   cup celery, chopped
  ¼   cup parsley, chopped
  2   to 3 cups turkey broth
      Salt and pepper

Simmer neck and giblets in water with celery, onion, and bay leaf. Add salt and pepper to taste. Cook until tender (about 1 hour). Drain, reserving broth. Discard celery, onion, and bay leaf.

For roux: In a heavy saucepan, melt 2 tablespoons butter. Remove from heat; blend in flour and return to heat. Stirring slowly, cook over medium heat for 2 minutes. Remove from heat; set aside.

Sauté onion, celery, and parsley in remaining butter. Combine vegetables with cooked roux. Blend in broth and cook over medium heat, stirring constantly until gravy thickens. Chop giblets and meat from neck; add to gravy. Add salt and pepper to taste.

Yield: 5 cups

This luscious English Trifle looks as though it were created by a master chef, but it's actually simple to make with layers of pound cake, custard, raspberries, and brandy-laced almond macaroons.

CORNBREAD DRESSING

CORNBREAD

  2   cups cornmeal
  ½   cup flour
  3   teaspoons baking powder
  1   teaspoon sugar
  1¼ teaspoons salt
  3   eggs
  1   cup milk
  4   tablespoons butter, melted

Combine cornmeal, flour, baking powder, sugar, and salt. Beat in eggs and milk. Add butter and beat again.

Pour mixture into greased 9-inch baking pan or cast-iron skillet. Bake in a preheated 425 degree oven for 30 to 35 minutes or until golden brown. Cornbread may be made ahead and frozen.

DRESSING

  ½   cup butter
  ⅓   cup turkey broth
  1½ cups celery, chopped
  1   cup onion, chopped
      Cornbread, crumbled
  ½   cup bread crumbs, toasted
  ½   cup saltine crackers, crumbled
  1½ teaspoons marjoram
  ½   teaspoon thyme
  5   to 6 eggs, beaten
      Salt and pepper
      Turkey broth (chicken broth may be
        used)

In a saucepan, melt butter; add ⅓ cup broth, celery, and onion. Sauté over medium heat until vegetables are soft.

In a large bowl, combine crumbled cornbread, bread crumbs, crackers, and vegetables. Add marjoram and thyme; mix lightly.

Beat eggs; stir into dressing. Add salt and pepper to taste. Dressing mixture should be very moist; add more broth if necessary. Pour into a greased 9 x 13-inch baking pan. Bake in a preheated 350 degree oven for 45 to 60 minutes.

Yield: 10 to 12 servings

ENGLISH TRIFLE

This is a perfect holiday recipe — rich custard combined with brandy-laced almond macaroons. You can make this ahead of time and then sit down and enjoy this treat with the family on Christmas Day.

  8   eggs
  6   tablespoons sugar
  5   teaspoons cornstarch
  4   cups milk, scalded
  1   teaspoon vanilla
  ¼   teaspoon nutmeg, freshly grated
  20 (2-inch) almond macaroons
  ⅓   cup brandy
  1   (12-ounce) jar red raspberry jam
  1   (12-ounce) pound cake, cut into
        ¼-inch thick slices
  ½   cup cream sherry
  4   (10-ounce) packages frozen
        raspberries, thawed and drained
  2   cups heavy cream
  2   tablespoons sugar
  ½   teaspoon vanilla

For custard: In a heavy saucepan or double boiler, whisk eggs. Blend 6 tablespoons sugar and cornstarch; add to eggs, blending well. Pour scalded milk into mixture in a steady stream, stirring constantly. Cook mixture over medium heat, stirring until thickened (5 to 6 minutes). Remove from heat and add vanilla and nutmeg. Set aside to cool.

Brush all the cookies with brandy. Line the bottom of a 12-cup glass serving bowl with a single layer of cookies. Spread flat side of additional cookies with jam and arrange in one layer around the sides of bowl (jam side out). Coat all cookies with another generous layer of jam.

Spoon a portion of custard over jam layer. Arrange one-half of cake slices over custard. Carefully brush cake with about ¼ cup sherry. Spread jam over cake. Add a layer of raspberries. Repeat layers of custard, cake slices, sherry, and jam. Cover with raspberries and top with remaining custard. Place remaining cookies in center of the dessert, flat side down. Cover tightly and refrigerate overnight.

Before serving, whip cream; add sugar and vanilla. Spoon over cookies. Garnish with fresh strawberries.

Yield: 10 to 12 servings

MERRY COUNTRY BRUNCH

A Merry Country Brunch is a delicious way to start the day — or the New Year! Full of country goodness and holiday flavor, this hearty fare is designed to wake up your appetite. Festive fruit adds delightful color and taste to a spirited punch, a rich ambrosia, and sweet baked goods. At the heart of the meal are a tasty egg casserole and some out-of-the-ordinary vegetables. Many of the foods can be prepared ahead of time, allowing you to enjoy the company of your guests with only a few last-minute preparations. This menu serves twelve.

Orange Ambrosia with Holiday Wine Sauce

Brunch Eggs

Tomatoes Stuffed with Spinach and Artichokes

Broccoli Roulade with Ham

Sugar Bacon

Apricot Conserve

Pumpkin Yeast Biscuits

Sweet Potato Muffins

Cranberry Breakfast Ring

Gingerbread with Lemon Custard Ice Cream

Christmas Snowball

Golden Breakfast Punch

MERRY COUNTRY BRUNCH

BRUNCH EGGS

- ½ cup butter
- 1 cup green onions, minced, including tops
- ¼ cup flour
- 2½ cups milk
- 1 cup sharp Cheddar cheese, grated
- ¼ cup sherry
- ¾ teaspoon seasoned salt
- ¼ teaspoon curry powder
- ¼ teaspoon white pepper
- ¼ teaspoon cayenne pepper
- ½ teaspoon dry mustard
- 18 eggs
- 1 cup water
- 2 tablespoons oil
  Salt and pepper
- ½ cup green onions, chopped, including tops

In a saucepan, melt ¼ cup butter. Add minced onions and sauté until soft. Remove from heat and blend in flour. Stirring slowly, cook over moderate heat for 2 minutes. Remove from heat; gradually add milk. Return to heat and cook until thickened. Add cheese and stir. Remove from heat; add sherry and seasonings. Cool.

Beat eggs with water. Scramble eggs in remaining butter and oil until barely set. Salt and pepper to taste.

Butter two 2-quart casseroles. Pour small amount of sauce into bottoms of casseroles. Spoon scrambled eggs into casseroles and cover with remainder of sauce. If the casseroles are being made in advance, cover tightly and refrigerate until ready to bake. (It is important that eggs be completely covered with sauce.)

When ready to serve, bring casseroles to room temperature and bake, covered, in a preheated 275 degree oven for 1 hour. Keep eggs warm over hot water until ready to serve. Sprinkle with chopped green onions.

Yield: 12 servings

GOLDEN BREAKFAST PUNCH

We decorated our punch with an ice ring garnished with fresh herb leaves and kumquats.

- 2 tea bags
- 2 cups boiling water
- 1½ to 2 cups sugar
- 3 cups orange juice, freshly squeezed
- 2 cups lemon juice, freshly squeezed
- 1 quart dry white wine
- 1 cup vodka

Place tea bags in boiling water and steep 5 minutes. Remove tea bags. Add sugar and juices; stir until sugar is dissolved. Cool. Add wine and vodka; chill. Serve over ice ring in punch bowl or in glasses filled with ice.

Yield: 3 quarts

TOMATOES STUFFED WITH SPINACH AND ARTICHOKES

- 6 large tomatoes
- ½ cup green onions, chopped, including tops
- ½ cup butter or margarine
- 2 (10-ounce) packages frozen chopped spinach
  Salt
- 1 (14-ounce) can artichoke hearts, drained and chopped
- 1 teaspoon Worcestershire sauce
- 3 dashes Tabasco® sauce
- 1 cup sour cream
- ¾ cup Parmesan cheese, grated
- 3 tablespoons butter or margarine

Wash tomatoes, remove stems, and scoop out seeds; turn upside down to drain.

In a large skillet, sauté onions in ½ cup butter.

Cook spinach; lightly salt and drain. Add spinach, artichoke hearts, Worcestershire, Tabasco®, and sour cream to onions. Stir in ½ cup cheese.

Stuff tomatoes with spinach mixture and sprinkle with remaining cheese; dot with butter. Bake in a preheated 350 degree oven for 20 minutes or until thoroughly heated.

Yield: 6 servings

BROCCOLI ROULADE WITH HAM

- 4 (10-ounce) packages frozen chopped broccoli
- ½ cup dry bread crumbs
  Pinch of nutmeg
- 6 tablespoons butter, melted
  Salt and pepper
- 4 eggs, separated
- 8 tablespoons Parmesan cheese, grated
  Creamed Ham (recipe follows)

Cook broccoli according to package directions. Cool and finely chop.

Butter a 10½ x 15½ x 1-inch baking pan and line with waxed paper. Butter waxed paper well and sprinkle with bread crumbs.

In a large mixing bowl, combine the broccoli, nutmeg, and butter; salt and pepper to taste. Beat in egg yolks, one at a time, blending thoroughly after each addition.

Beat the egg whites until soft peaks are formed; fold into broccoli mixture. Turn into prepared pan and smooth top with rubber spatula. Sprinkle with 4 tablespoons cheese.

Bake in a preheated 350 degree oven for 12 to 16 minutes, or until center feels barely firm when touched.

Place a sheet of buttered waxed paper over the top of the broccoli mixture and invert onto a large baking sheet. Carefully peel away waxed paper. Spread Creamed Ham over broccoli mixture. Beginning with long side, gently roll up broccoli mixture. Sprinkle with remaining cheese.

Yield: 12 servings

CREAMED HAM

- 3 tablespoons butter
- 3 tablespoons flour
- ¾ cup chicken broth
- 1 teaspoon Dijon mustard
- 2 tablespoons sherry
  Salt and pepper
- ½ cup light cream
- 1½ cups boiled or baked ham, diced
- 1 (4-ounce) can sliced mushrooms, drained

In a saucepan, melt butter. Remove from heat and add flour. Stirring slowly, cook over moderate heat for 2 minutes. Remove from heat; gradually stir in broth, mustard, and sherry. Salt and pepper to taste. Return to heat and cook until mixture thickens. Add cream, ham, and mushrooms; continue cooking until thoroughly heated.

(Top) Our spirited Golden Breakfast Punch is a tangy combination of tea and freshly squeezed fruit juices. We kept it frosty cold with a colorful ice ring made with kumquats and herbs, then served it in canning jars to bring an authentic country touch to the table.

(Bottom) This hearty fare is designed to satisfy country-style appetites: *(clockwise from top)* Brunch Eggs, Tomatoes Stuffed with Spinach and Artichokes, and Broccoli Roulade with Ham.

HELPFUL HINTS

For tender, moist **Sweet Potato Muffins**, *use a gentle hand when mixing batter. Overmixing causes quick breads to have a coarse texture.*

To speed up the rising time of bread dough, place your bowl of dough in a cold oven over a pan of warm water.

Small jars of **Apricot Conserve** *make wonderful party favors for your guests to take home. Prepare several recipes; fill jars and decorate with bows.*

SWEET POTATO MUFFINS

    2 cups flour, sifted
    2 teaspoons baking powder
  ½ teaspoon soda
    1 teaspoon salt
  1¼ teaspoons cinnamon
  ½ teaspoon nutmeg
    1 cup cooked sweet potatoes, mashed
    1 cup sugar
  ½ cup milk
    2 eggs
  ¼ cup butter, melted
  ¾ cup pecans, chopped

Sift together flour, baking powder, soda, salt, cinnamon, and nutmeg; set aside. In a mixing bowl, combine sweet potatoes, sugar, milk, and eggs. Add dry ingredients and butter; mix until well blended. Stir in nuts. Fill greased muffin cups one-half full. Bake in a preheated 350 degree oven for 20 minutes. The muffins are done when a wooden pick inserted in the center comes out clean.
Yield: 24 muffins

SUGAR BACON

    5 teaspoons prepared mustard
  10 teaspoons Worcestershire sauce
  ½ cup light brown sugar, firmly packed
    4 egg yolks
  20 thin slices bacon
    2 cups fine bread crumbs

Beat mustard, Worcestershire, sugar, and egg yolks together. Dip bacon in mixture and roll in crumbs. Place bacon in a broiler pan. Bake in a preheated 250 degree oven for 20 minutes or until brown and crispy.
Yield: 20 slices

A delicious Cranberry Breakfast Ring adds a festive touch to the table. For munching, there are Sweet Potato Muffins and Pumpkin Yeast Biscuits filled with slices of smoked turkey.

PUMPKIN YEAST BISCUITS

We filled our biscuits with slivers of smoked turkey. You could also use country ham or thin sausage patties.

    2 (¼-ounce) packages dry yeast
  ½ teaspoon sugar
  ½ cup warm water
  ½ cup butter, melted
    1 cup milk, scalded and cooled
    1 cup canned pumpkin, mashed
    1 cup light brown sugar, firmly packed
  6 to 7 cups flour
    2 teaspoons salt
    2 teaspoons pumpkin pie spice
    1 teaspoon ground ginger

Dissolve yeast and ½ teaspoon sugar in warm water. Let stand until bubbly.
In a large mixing bowl, combine yeast mixture, butter, milk, pumpkin, and brown sugar. Add flour, salt, and seasonings. Stir until soft dough forms. Knead on a floured surface until dough is smooth and elastic (about 10 to 12 minutes).
Place dough in a greased bowl, turning to coat. Cover and let rise until double in size (about 2 to 3 hours).
On a lightly floured surface, roll dough to ½-inch thickness. Cut out biscuits with a floured 1½-inch round cutter.
Grease a baking sheet and arrange biscuits close together on sheet. Cover and let rise until double in size (about 1 hour).
Bake in a preheated 350 degree oven for 25 minutes or until golden brown.
Yield: 50 biscuits

APRICOT CONSERVE

    1 (6-ounce) package dried apricots
  ½ cup slivered almonds, chopped
  ½ cup golden raisins
  ½ teaspoon cinnamon
    1 cup sugar

Cover apricots with water and soak overnight; drain. In a saucepan, mix apricots with remaining ingredients. Stir mixture over low heat until sugar is dissolved. Cook slowly until thickened, stirring often. Cool and store in refrigerator.
Yield: 1 pint

CRANBERRY BREAKFAST RING

Our pretty breakfast ring makes a yummy gift to a special friend. Wrap tightly and freeze if making in advance.

    2 (¼-ounce) packages dry yeast
  3½ to 4½ cups flour
  ½ cup sugar
    1 teaspoon salt
    1 cup milk
  ¼ cup water
  ½ cup butter or margarine
    2 eggs, beaten
    1 teaspoon lemon rind, grated
    1 (14-ounce) jar cranberry orange sauce
  ¾ cup sugar
    1 cup walnuts, chopped
    2 teaspoons cinnamon
  ½ cup butter or margarine, melted
       Frosting (recipe follows)

In a large bowl, combine yeast, 1¼ cups flour, ½ cup sugar, and salt. Set aside.
In a saucepan, combine milk, water, and butter; heat until warm. Add to dry ingredients and beat until smooth. Add eggs and 1¼ cups flour, beating again until mixed. Stir in remaining flour and lemon rind. Cover and refrigerate until ready to shape rings.
To make rings, turn dough onto floured board and divide in half. Roll one-half into a 14 x 7-inch rectangle. Spread one-half of cranberry orange sauce over dough. Combine sugar, nuts, and cinnamon; sprinkle one-half of mixture over dough. Drizzle with ¼ cup melted butter. Beginning with one long side, roll up dough and seal edges. With seam edge down, place dough in a circle on a greased baking sheet. Press ends together to seal. Cut slits two-thirds of the way through ring at 1-inch intervals. Repeat process with remaining half of dough. Cover rings and let rise in a warm place until double in size (about 1 hour).
Bake in a preheated 375 degree oven 20 to 25 minutes or until done. Bread is done when you thump the ring and it makes a hollow sound, not a thud. Frost if desired.
Yield: 2 rings

FROSTING

    1 cup confectioners' sugar
    2 tablespoons warm milk
  ½ teaspoon vanilla
Mix all ingredients until smooth; drizzle over rings.

145

MERRY COUNTRY BRUNCH

HELPFUL HINTS

Spicy **Gingerbread** *is a favorite at Christmastime. Do not use a substitute for the molasses and be sure the water is boiling when you add it to your batter.*

Peel and slice the oranges for our **Orange Ambrosia with Holiday Wine Sauce** *the day before your party. Toast the coconut ahead of time. Store the oranges and the coconut in separate airtight containers until ready to use.*

GINGERBREAD WITH LEMON CUSTARD ICE CREAM

- ½ cup shortening
- ½ cup sugar
- 1 egg
- 2½ cups flour
- ½ teaspoon salt
- 1 teaspoon ginger
- 1 teaspoon allspice
- 1 teaspoon cloves
- 1 teaspoon cinnamon
- 1 teaspoon baking powder
- 2 tablespoons orange rind, freshly grated
- 1 cup molasses
- 1 cup boiling water
  Lemon Custard Ice Cream

In a large mixing bowl, cream shortening and sugar until well blended. Add egg and beat. Sift dry ingredients together; add to creamed mixture, blending well.

Add orange rind, molasses, and water; stir just enough to blend ingredients. Pour into a greased and floured 9 x 12-inch pan or a 10-inch ring mold. Bake in a preheated 375 degree oven for 30 minutes. Cool before unmolding. Serve with ice cream.

Yield: 12 servings

(Top) Delight the chocolate lovers at your brunch with a Christmas Snowball. Underneath its whipped cream frosting is a magnificently rich chocolate dessert that will melt in your mouth.

(Bottom left) Gingerbread with Lemon Custard Ice Cream is a luscious ending for a holiday party. When you bake this spicy dessert in a ring mold, you can serve the ice cream from a crock placed inside the ring.

(Bottom right) Orange Ambrosia with Holiday Wine Sauce adds heavenly flavor to a meal.

CHRISTMAS SNOWBALL

A chocolate lover's delight. Our snowball is a dazzling, rich chocolate dessert decorated with Whipped Cream Frosting and Chocolate Leaves.

- 8 (1-ounce) squares semisweet chocolate
- ½ cup boiling water
- 1 teaspoon vanilla
- 1 cup sugar
- 1 cup unsalted butter, softened
- 4 large eggs
  Whipped Cream Frosting (recipe follows)
  Chocolate Leaves (recipe follows)

Preheat oven to 350 degrees. Oven rack should be placed one third up from the bottom of oven. Line a deep, narrow, oven-proof bowl (6 to 8 cups) with foil.

In a small saucepan, melt chocolate. Add boiling water, vanilla, and sugar; stir until well blended.

Pour mixture into a large mixing bowl and beat until smooth. Add butter, a few tablespoons at a time; beat until creamy. Add eggs, one at a time, beating after each egg.

Spoon mixture into foil-lined bowl and bake about one hour. When done, the top will be cracked, puffy, and firm when touched. While chocolate is cooling, a hollow will form in the center. Gently press sides down, allowing the surface to flatten.

When completely cool, wrap tightly with foil and refrigerate overnight (at this point it can be frozen).

Several hours before serving, remove foil and invert dessert on a serving plate. Decorate with Whipped Cream Frosting and Chocolate Leaves. Refrigerate until ready to serve.

Yield: 12 servings

WHIPPED CREAM FROSTING

- 1½ teaspoons unflavored gelatin
- 1½ tablespoons cold water
- 2½ cups heavy cream, reserve ¼ cup
- ⅓ cup confectioners' sugar
- 1 teaspoon vanilla

In a small bowl, blend gelatin with water. Let stand 5 minutes to completely dissolve.

In a small bowl, use an electric mixer to beat 2¼ cups cream, sugar, and vanilla until soft peaks form. Combine remaining cream with gelatin mixture. Reduce mixer speed to medium and gradually add gelatin mixture. Frosting should be creamy and firm enough to hold a shape when dropped from a spoon.

CHOCOLATE LEAVES

- 5 or 6 fresh leaves, such as rose, ivy, or lemon leaves (leaves should be firm, with raised veins on the underside)
- 1 (1-ounce) square semisweet chocolate

Wash and dry leaves thoroughly; set aside.

Chop chocolate and place in a small double boiler. Melt over hot (not boiling) water. Remove chocolate from water.

Holding leaf by the stem, use a small brush to coat underside of leaf with chocolate. Be careful not to let chocolate run to the front of the leaf. Place leaf, chocolate side up, on a tray; repeat for desired number of leaves. Place in freezer to harden.

After chocolate is firm, carefully peel away leaves. Return chocolate leaves to freezer until ready to decorate Snowball.

ORANGE AMBROSIA WITH HOLIDAY WINE SAUCE

- 10 to 12 oranges, peeled and sliced
- 1 cup shredded coconut, lightly toasted
- 2 (4-ounce) packages instant vanilla pudding mix
- 1⅓ cups milk
- 1 cup orange juice, freshly squeezed and chilled
- ½ cup sherry
- 1 cup heavy cream, whipped
  Grated rind of 1 fresh orange

Layer orange slices and coconut in a large serving bowl.

For wine sauce: Combine pudding mix, milk, orange juice, and sherry. Beat until smooth. Set aside for 5 minutes. Fold in cream and orange rind. Sauce may be poured over fruit mixture or served in a separate bowl.

Yield: 12 servings

HOLIDAY OPEN HOUSE

When you want to bring friends and neighbors together for a round of Christmas cheer, a Holiday Open House is the answer. To help you, we've assembled a variety of foods that will please those who bring a big appetite, as well as those who just want to munch while they mingle. There are crisp appetizers, savory meats, spicy vegetables, and luscious desserts — all beautiful, delicious foods that lend themselves to casual, stand-up dining. Make plans now to fill your home with good friends and good things to eat — you'll have a good time!

Spicy Pecans

Sugared Walnuts

Spice Cheese Mold

Monterey Cheese Crisps

Party Cheese Rolls

Cold Shrimp, Artichokes, and Mushrooms

Burgundy Mushrooms

Glazed Ginger Pork

Marmalade Meatballs

Oysters Creole in Peppered Pastry Shells

Smoked Oyster Roll

Bourbon Pecan Balls

Fruity Pudding Cake

Floating Holiday Dessert

Southern Eggnog

Wine Cooler

GLAZED GINGER PORK

Cooked ahead and served cold, this ginger-flavored pork is an easy dish for entertaining.

- ¼ cup soy sauce
- ¼ cup dry white wine
- 1 tablespoon ginger, freshly grated
- 2 tablespoons honey
- 1 garlic clove, minced
- 1 (3-pound) pork loin roast, boneless
- ¾ cup currant jelly

For marinade: In a container, combine soy sauce, wine, ginger, honey, and garlic. Place roast in marinade. Cover and marinate roast in the refrigerator for 6 hours or overnight, turning several times.

When ready to cook, remove roast from container and place on a rack in a shallow baking pan. Reserve 3 to 4 tablespoons of marinade for glaze; the remainder will be for basting. Bake in a preheated 300 degree oven for 2 hours or until meat thermometer inserted in roast reaches 175 degrees. Baste several times with marinade during cooking.

For glaze: In a saucepan, combine 3 to 4 tablespoons reserved marinade with jelly. Cook over low heat until jelly is dissolved. Set aside to cool.

After the roast is cooked, spoon glaze over the meat until it is completely coated. Refrigerate until ready to serve. Slice roast paper thin. Serve with sweet mustard and assorted breads.
Yield: 50 slices

(Top) Tangy Glazed Ginger Pork and Marmalade Meatballs will keep your guests coming back for more.

(Bottom left) Jalapeno peppers and spicy hot pecans add exciting taste to our Spice Cheese Mold.

(Bottom right) Meet the call for crunchies with Monterey Cheese Crisps *(clockwise from top)*, Sugared Walnuts, and Spicy Pecans. Our festive Wine Coolers offer fruity flavor.

MARMALADE MEATBALLS

Bake these in batches and freeze for a holiday party.

- 1 egg
- ½ cup water
- 1 pound ground chuck, twice ground
- ½ cup bread crumbs
- ¼ teaspoon salt
- 2 teaspoons horseradish
- 1 cup water chestnuts, finely chopped
- ⅔ cup orange marmalade
- 1 garlic clove, finely minced
- 2 tablespoons soy sauce
- 2 tablespoons lemon juice
- ⅓ cup water

In a medium bowl, beat egg and ½ cup water. Blend in ground chuck, crumbs, salt, horseradish, and chestnuts. (**Note:** For tender meatballs, do not over blend.) Shape mixture into balls about ¾ inch in diameter. Place meatballs on a foil-lined baking sheet. Bake in a preheated 350 degree oven for 30 minutes or until lightly browned.

While meatballs are cooking, make sauce by combining remaining ingredients in a saucepan. Heat slowly, stirring often.

Place cooked meatballs in a serving dish and cover with sauce. If making in advance, place meatballs and sauce in a covered container and refrigerate. Heat slowly before serving.
Yield: 24 servings

SPICE CHEESE MOLD

A blend of cheeses with the bite of jalapeno peppers and hot-flavored pecans.

- 2 (8-ounce) packages cream cheese, softened
- 8 ounces sharp Cheddar cheese, softened
- 8 ounces Monterey Jack cheese with jalapeno peppers, softened
- 3 dashes Tabasco® sauce
- 1¼ cups Spicy Pecans (recipe on this page)

In a food processor or blender, combine cheeses and Tabasco®. Process until well blended. Place mixture in a bowl and add ¾ cup chopped Spicy Pecans. Form into a large ball or mold in a 1-quart round bowl. Cover tightly and refrigerate overnight. When ready to serve, remove from refrigerator and garnish with remaining Spicy Pecans. Serve with fresh grapes and assorted crackers.
Yield: 24 servings

SUGARED WALNUTS

A brown sugar coating makes these crispy nuts a sweet treat for the holidays.

- 8 cups water
- 4 cups English walnut halves
- ½ cup light brown sugar, firmly packed
  Vegetable oil
  Salt

In a large pan, bring water to a boil. Add walnuts and boil for 1 minute. Drain nuts and rinse in very hot water; drain again. Place warm nuts in a bowl and add sugar. Stir until sugar is melted.

In a heavy skillet, heat 1 inch of oil to 320 degrees on a candy thermometer. Cook 2 cups of nuts at a time for 3 to 4 minutes. (Do not overcook.) Drain on paper towels. Store in airtight containers.
Yield: 4 cups

MONTEREY CHEESE CRISPS

You won't believe how easy these are to make. A sprinkle of cayenne pepper gives them an added bite.

- 1 pound Monterey Jack cheese, softened (use only Monterey Jack cheese)
  Cayenne pepper or chili powder

Cut cheese into ¼-inch thick slices, then cut slices into circles, using a 1½-inch round cookie cutter. Place cheese rounds 3 inches apart on a non-stick baking sheet (cheese will spread while baking). Sprinkle with cayenne or chili powder.

Bake in a preheated 400 degree oven for 10 minutes or until golden brown. (Do not overbake.)

Remove crisps with a spatula and cool on paper towels. Store in airtight containers.
Yield: 36 to 42 crisps

SPICY PECANS

Your guests will beg for more of these, so bake plenty to serve and to give to friends.

- ½ cup butter
- 3 tablespoons A-1® steak sauce
- 6 dashes Tabasco® sauce
- 4 cups pecan halves
  Cajun seasoning

Melt butter in a large baking sheet in a preheated 200 degree oven. Add steak sauce and Tabasco®; stir in nuts. Spread nuts out on baking sheet and bake for 1 hour. Stir often while baking. Drain on paper towels and sprinkle with Cajun seasoning. Store in airtight containers.
Yield: 4 cups

HOLIDAY OPEN HOUSE

OYSTERS CREOLE IN PEPPERED PASTRY SHELLS

An authentic Cajun Country recipe. Fresh oysters are cooked with lots of chopped vegetables and seasoned the way they are down South.

    4 (10-ounce) jars fresh oysters, drained,
         reserving liquor
    ⅓ cup butter
    1 cup celery, minced
    1 cup parsley, minced
    ½ cup onion, minced
    ½ cup green onions, minced, including
         tops
    1 cup green pepper, minced
    1 cup cracker crumbs
    ½ teaspoon salt
    ¾ teaspoon Cajun seasoning
    ½ teaspoon pepper
    ¼ teaspoon cayenne pepper
    2 eggs, beaten
    1½ tablespoons Worcestershire sauce
    5 tablespoons catsup
       Peppered Pastry Shells (recipe follows)

Chop oysters and set aside.

In a large skillet, melt butter and add vegetables. Sauté until tender. Add ½ cup reserved oyster liquor to vegetables and cook slowly until all liquid has evaporated. While vegetables are cooking, blend cracker crumbs with remaining oyster liquor. Set aside.

In a saucepan, combine vegetables, crumbs, salt, Cajun seasoning, pepper, and cayenne. Add eggs; blend well. Cook over low heat for 25 minutes. Add oysters, Worcestershire, and catsup. Cook 5 more minutes. Serve hot in Peppered Pastry Shells.

Yield: 25 servings

PEPPERED PASTRY SHELLS

    1 (3-ounce) package cream cheese,
         softened
    ½ cup butter, softened
    1 cup flour
    ½ teaspoon white pepper

In a small mixing bowl, blend cheese and butter. Combine flour and pepper; add to cheese mixture. Blend mixture with a fork until a ball forms. Cover with waxed paper and chill for 2 hours.

Roll out dough on a floured surface to ⅛-inch thickness. Cut out dough with a 3-inch round pastry cutter. Press dough into 1½ to 2½ -inch fluted tart pans. Trim any excess dough with a sharp knife. Prick bottom of dough with a fork.

Place tarts on a baking sheet. Bake in a preheated 425 degree oven for 10 to 12 minutes. Turn out of pans and cool completely on wire racks. Store in airtight containers or freeze until ready to use.

Yield: 30 to 32 shells

SOUTHERN EGGNOG

You will love our eggnog. It begins with a cooked custard made in advance. We also have included a version for those who prefer a non-spirited eggnog.

    1 cup sugar
    12 large eggs, separated
    ½ teaspoon salt
    1 quart milk
    2 cups heavy cream
    ½ cup brandy
    ½ cup dark rum
       Nutmeg, freshly grated

In a large double boiler, blend ½ cup sugar with the egg yolks and salt. Gradually stir in milk. Cook over simmering water until thickened and mixture coats the back of a metal spoon. Remove from heat and cool. Store mixture in refrigerator until thoroughly chilled.

Before serving, whip egg whites in a large bowl until stiff peaks form. Beat in remainder of sugar.

In a mixing bowl, whip cream until stiff peaks form.

Pour chilled mixture into a large punch bowl. Blend in brandy and rum. Fold in egg whites and cream. Sprinkle with nutmeg.

(**Note:** For a non-spirited eggnog, omit brandy and rum; stir 2 teaspoons rum extract and 1 cup cream into mixture. Sprinkle with nutmeg.)

Yield: approx. 3 quarts

WINE COOLER

    1 gallon red Zinfandel wine
    1 quart orange juice
    1 cup lemon juice
    ½ cup sugar
    1 quart club soda, chilled

In a large container, combine wine, juices, and sugar. Stir until sugar is dissolved. Chill completely.

When ready to serve, add club soda. Serve over ice with a slice of orange.

Yield: 1½ gallons

Oysters Creole, featuring lots of tender, spicy vegetables, is served hot in Peppered Pastry Shells.

BURGUNDY MUSHROOMS

These delicious butter-flavored mushrooms are simmered all day. They can be frozen in small containers and heated when friends drop in.

1½ cups butter
 1 quart red wine (a medium-priced burgundy is best)
 2 tablespoons Worcestershire sauce
 1 teaspoon dill seed
 1 teaspoon pepper
 1 teaspoon garlic powder
 2 cups boiling water
 3 beef bouillon cubes
 3 chicken bouillon cubes
 4 pounds fresh mushrooms
   Salt

In a large dutch oven, combine butter, wine, Worcestershire, dill, pepper, garlic, water, and bouillon; bring to a boil.

Clean mushrooms with a damp paper towel and trim ends of stems. Add mushrooms to liquid and reduce heat to simmer. Cover and cook 5 to 6 hours. Remove lid and cook 4 more hours. When ready, liquid should just cover mushrooms. Salt to taste. Serve hot.

Yield: 12 to 16 servings

(Top) Burgundy Mushrooms *(clockwise from top)*, Smoked Oyster Roll, and Party Cheese Rolls are delicious for nibbling.

(Bottom left) A medley of Cold Shrimp, Artichokes, and Mushrooms is seasoned with a spicy marinade.

(Bottom right) A holiday party isn't complete without sumptuous treats like these: *(clockwise from top right)* Fruity Pudding Cake, Bourbon Pecan Balls, Floating Holiday Dessert, and Southern Eggnog.

PARTY CHEESE ROLLS

Children and adults love these easy-to-prepare rolls. Make several recipes and freeze.

 5 dozen small finger rolls (about 2½-inch length)
 8 ounces sharp Cheddar cheese, grated
 8 ounces mild Cheddar cheese, grated
 1 (4¼-ounce) can ripe olives, chopped
 6 eggs, hard cooked and chopped
 1 (4-ounce) can green chilies, chopped
 1 cup tomato sauce
 1 teaspoon celery salt
 1 medium onion, finely chopped
 1 cup butter, softened

Split rolls in half. Using a small spoon, scoop out centers of rolls; reserve one-half of the crumbs.

Mix remaining ingredients together; add reserved crumbs. Stuff rolls with mixture. Bake in a preheated 400 degree oven for 10 to 15 minutes. Serve immediately.

Rolls can be placed in an airtight container and frozen before baking. To bake after freezing, thaw completely, wrap in foil, and heat.

Yield: 60 rolls

SMOKED OYSTER ROLL

This roll of flavor-filled smoked oysters wrapped in savory cream cheese keeps well in the refrigerator for days.

2½ tablespoons mayonnaise
 2 (8-ounce) packages cream cheese, softened
 2 teaspoons Worcestershire sauce
 2 garlic cloves, pressed
 1 tablespoon onion, finely minced
 2 (3¾-ounce) cans smoked oysters, drained and chopped

Cream mayonnaise with cheese. Add Worcestershire, garlic, and onion. Blend until smooth.

On a large sheet of foil, spread mixture into a 12 x 9-inch rectangle (about ½-inch thick). Place in the refrigerator until mixture begins to set. Remove from refrigerator and spread oysters on top of mixture.

Beginning with one long side, gently roll up mixture. Wrap tightly and chill for 24 hours. Remove foil and garnish with chives and parsley. Serve with assorted crackers.

Yield: 12 to 14 servings

COLD SHRIMP, ARTICHOKES, AND MUSHROOMS

This tangy-flavored combination is prepared 2 to 3 days before serving.

 7 to 8 pounds shrimp, boiled, peeled, and deveined
 1 pound fresh mushrooms, sliced
 3 (14-ounce) cans artichoke hearts, drained and halved
 2 cups olive oil
 2 cups vegetable oil
 1 cup dry sherry
 1 cup Garlic Vinegar (recipe on page 115)
 1 teaspoon salt
¼ teaspoon cayenne pepper
¾ tablespoon Cajun seasoning
¾ tablespoon Tabasco® sauce (optional)
 6 small purple onions, thinly sliced

In a large glass bowl, combine shrimp, mushrooms, and artichokes.

In another bowl, combine remaining ingredients (except onions). Whisk until blended. Pour over shrimp mixture. Cover tightly and refrigerate for 2 to 3 days, stirring occasionally. Several hours before serving, add onions. Place in a glass serving dish.

Yield: 60 servings

BOURBON PECAN BALLS

A sweet treat with the taste of bourbon and a coating of dark chocolate. Make several batches and freeze. Great gift idea from your kitchen.

 2 cups pecans, chopped
¾ cup bourbon
½ cup butter or margarine, softened
 1 teaspoon vanilla
2½ to 3 pounds confectioners' sugar
 4 (1-ounce) squares unsweetened chocolate
¼ bar paraffin

Place nuts in a jar and add bourbon. Place lid on jar and soak nuts for two days; stir occasionally.

In a large mixing bowl, blend butter and vanilla; add nuts. Gradually add sugar until mixture is stiff. Cover mixture and chill overnight.

Shape mixture into ¾-inch balls. Place balls on baking sheets and cover tightly. (**Note:** Balls should be chilled or frozen to be firm enough to hold a shape when dipped into chocolate.)

In a small double boiler, melt chocolate and paraffin. Stir until smooth. Use a wooden pick to dip balls in chocolate. Lay balls on waxed paper to harden. Store in refrigerator or freeze.

Yield: approx. 100 balls

FLOATING HOLIDAY DESSERT

Raspberry sauce adds elegance to this brandied coconut dessert.

- ¾ cup sugar
- ⅓ cup water
- 3 egg yolks
  Dash salt
- 1 cup coconut macaroons, crumbled
- 5 ladyfingers, split
- 2 tablespoons brandy
- 1½ cups heavy cream
- 2 teaspoons vanilla
- ½ teaspoon almond extract
  Raspberry Sauce (recipe follows)

In a small saucepan, combine sugar and water. Bring to a boil over medium heat and stir until sugar is dissolved. Continue to gently boil, without stirring, until mixture reaches 230 degrees on a candy thermometer. Sugar mixture will spin a thread when dropped from spoon. Remove from heat.

In a large mixing bowl, combine egg yolks with salt and beat until light. Gradually add hot syrup, pouring in a thin stream; beat until mixture begins to cool (about 2 minutes). Stir in macaroons. Place mixture in the refrigerator for 30 minutes.

Sprinkle ladyfingers with brandy; set aside.

In a mixing bowl, combine 1½ cups cream with flavorings; beat until stiff. With rubber spatula, fold whipped cream into macaroon mixture. Spray a 6-cup ring mold with vegetable spray until well coated. Turn half of mixture into mold; cover with ladyfingers and remaining mixture. Cover tightly and freeze until firm (about 4 hours).

When ready to serve, dip mold in hot water to loosen ring. Invert on a chilled shallow serving dish. Spoon Raspberry Sauce around dessert and serve.

Yield: 10 servings

RASPBERRY SAUCE

- ½ cup sugar
- ¼ cup water
- 1 (10-ounce) package frozen raspberries, thawed
- 2 tablespoons lemon juice
- 2 tablespoons Raspberry Liqueur (recipe on page 111)
- 2 teaspoons cornstarch
- 3 teaspoons water

In a saucepan, combine sugar and water. Bring to a boil over medium heat; stir until sugar is dissolved. Boil 2 minutes and remove from heat. Add raspberries, lemon juice, and liqueur. Return to heat and cook until well blended, stirring constantly. Dissolve cornstarch in water. Blend cornstarch mixture into raspberry mixture and stir until thickened. Remove from heat and cool. Store in refrigerator until ready to serve.

FRUITY PUDDING CAKE

Enjoy the convenience of packaged mixes in this holiday dessert. Fruits, nuts, and pudding combined with pineapple-flavored cake will become a family tradition.

- 1 (18¼-ounce) box pineapple cake mix
- 2 (3¾-ounce) packages vanilla pudding mix
- 1 (8¾-ounce) can crushed pineapple, drained
- ½ cup dates, chopped
- ½ cup canned apricots, drained and chopped
- ½ cup candied cherries, chopped
- ½ cup flaked coconut
- ½ cup brandy
- ¾ cup pecans, chopped
- 2½ cups heavy cream, whipped

Prepare cake batter according to package directions. Pour batter into a greased and floured 12 x 16-inch baking sheet. Bake in a preheated 350 degree oven for 25 minutes or until center is firm when touched. Cool on a wire rack.

Prepare pudding according to package directions. Cool completely and chill in the refrigerator for several hours.

Mix drained pineapple, dates, apricots, cherries, and coconut. Spoon 2 tablespoons brandy over mixture and drain. Combine fruit mixture with cold pudding. Add nuts and blend. Return to refrigerator until ready to assemble cake.

Cut cake in half (you will have two 12 x 8-inch pieces). Sprinkle remaining brandy over bottom layer of cake. Spread pudding over cake; place remaining layer of cake on top. Frost top with whipped cream. Garnish with glazed apricot pieces.

Yield: 20 servings

GENERAL INSTRUCTIONS

TRANSFERRING PATTERNS

When entire pattern is shown, place a piece of tracing paper over pattern and trace pattern, marking all placement symbols and openings. Cut out traced pattern.

When one-half of pattern is shown, fold tracing paper in half and place folded edge along dashed line of pattern. Trace pattern, marking all placement symbols and openings. Cut out traced pattern; open pattern and lay it flat.

SEWING SHAPES

Center pattern on wrong side of one piece of fabric and use a fabric marking pencil to draw around pattern. If indicated on pattern, mark opening for turning. **DO NOT CUT OUT SHAPE.** With right sides facing and leaving an opening for turning, carefully sew fabric pieces together **directly on pencil line.** Leaving a ¼ " seam allowance, cut out shape. Clip seam allowance at curves and corners. Turn shape right side out. Use the rounded end of a small crochet hook to completely turn small areas. If pattern has facial features or detail lines, use fabric marking pencil to lightly mark placement of features or lines.

WORKING ON LINEN

Using a hoop is optional when working on linen. To work without a hoop, roll the excess fabric from left to right until stitching area is in the proper position. Use the sewing method instead of the stab method to stitch over two fabric threads on the front of the fabric. To add support to stitches on linen, it is important to place the first Cross Stitch on fabric with stitch 1-2 beginning and ending where a vertical fabric thread crosses over a horizontal fabric thread (**Fig. 1**). When the first stitch is in the correct position, the entire design will be placed properly, with vertical fabric threads supporting each stitch.

Fig. 1

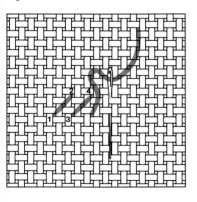

MAKING A MULTI-LOOP BOW

Hold ribbon in one hand with wrong side facing you, leaving a tail of ribbon above thumb. Loop ribbon over thumb, inserting it between thumb and tail of ribbon. Pinch ribbon together with thumb and index finger (**Fig. 1a**). Twist ribbon length and tail of ribbon so right sides are now facing you.

Fig. 1a

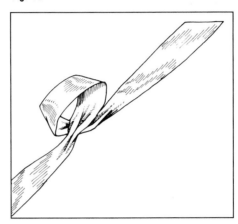

Make a second loop desired size; pinch ribbon together and twist. Make a third loop the same size as previous loop; pinch ribbon together and twist (**Fig. 1b**). Continue forming and twisting loops until desired fullness is reached. Insert a piece of florist wire through top loop, over center of bow. Bring ends of wire around to back of bow and twist tightly together.

Fig. 1b

CROSS STITCH

COUNTED CROSS STITCH

Work one Cross Stitch to correspond to each colored square on the chart. For horizontal rows, work stitches in two journeys (**Fig. 1**). For vertical rows, complete each stitch as shown (**Fig. 2**). When working over two fabric threads, work Cross Stitch as shown in **Fig. 3**. When the chart shows a Backstitch crossing a colored square (**Fig. 4**), a Cross Stitch (**Fig. 1, 2, or 3**) should be worked first; then the Backstitch (**Fig. 7**, page 158) should be worked on top of the Cross Stitch.

Fig. 1

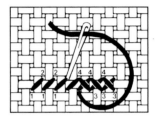

Fig. 2

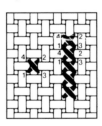

Fig. 3

Fig. 4

Continued on page 158.

QUARTER STITCHES (¼X and ¾X)

Quarter Stitches are denoted by triangular shapes of color on the chart and on the color key. Stitch 1-2 is the One-Quarter Stitch (¼X) (**Fig. 5**). When stitches 1-4 are worked in the same color, the resulting stitch is called a Three-Quarter Stitch (¾X). **Fig. 6** shows this technique when working over two fabric threads.

Fig. 5

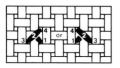

Fig. 6

BACKSTITCH

For outline detail, Backstitch (shown on chart and on color key by black or colored straight lines) should be worked after the design has been completed (**Fig. 7**).

Fig. 7

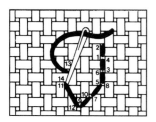

FRENCH KNOT

Bring needle up at 1. Wrap thread once around needle and insert needle at 2, holding end of thread with non-stitching fingers (**Fig. 8**). Tighten knot; then pull needle through fabric, holding thread until it must be released. For a larger knot, use more strands; wrap only once.

Fig. 8

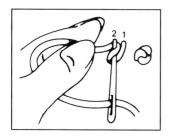

CROCHET

WORKING INTO THE CHAIN

When working into the beginning chain of a crochet project, insert hook **into the ridge** at back of each chain (**Fig. 1**).

Fig. 1

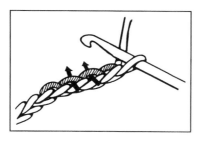

WORKING INTO ROWS

When working into rows of a crochet project, insert hook **under** the V of each stitch (**Fig. 2**). Be sure to pick up both loops.

Fig. 2

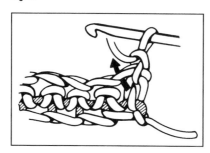

TURNING WORK

When a row has been completed on a crochet project, turn work counterclockwise (**Fig. 3**). It is possible to turn work clockwise, but the counterclockwise method gives a slight twist at the side, resulting in a firmer edge.

Fig. 3

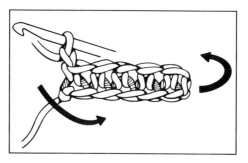

SINGLE CROCHET

To begin a single crochet, insert hook into ridge of chain or under V of stitch. Hook yarn and draw through (**Fig. 4**). There are now two loops on hook (**Fig. 5**). Hook yarn and draw through the two loops on hook. One single crochet is now complete.

Fig. 4

Fig. 5

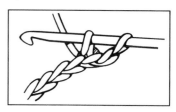

DOUBLE CROCHET

To begin a double crochet, wind yarn once over hook, remembering to bring yarn from back over top of hook. Insert hook into ridge of chain or under V of stitch. Hook yarn and draw through. There should now be three loops on hook (**Fig. 6**). Hook yarn again and draw through the first two loops on hook (**Fig. 7**). Two loops should remain on hook. Hook yarn again and draw through remaining two loops (**Fig. 8**). One double crochet is now complete.

Fig. 6

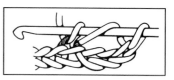

Fig. 7

Fig. 8

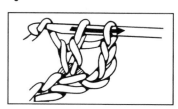

CREDITS

We wish to extend our heartfelt thanks to Florence Fee and Helen McQuiston for providing the old-fashioned Santas illustrating our cover and introductory pages. These talented ladies made the Santas using designs and techniques that they developed with the nostalgic collector in mind. The lifelike faces are hand-molded of clay made according to an old family recipe. ''We wanted them to be an heirloom, and this we found to be the most substantial,'' Mrs. McQuiston told us. Facial features are handpainted, and the wooden bodies are dressed with old clothing and laden with old-fashioned toys. They have made the Santas in 50 sizes ranging in height from 2 inches to 6 feet. The handwork and clothing give each one a unique personality, and by the time the Santas are finished, Mrs. Fee says she loves them all. She photographs each one before it's sold and sometimes keeps one or two that she can't bear to part with. For more information about the Santas, you may write to Florence Fee at 108 Countrywood, Covington, Tennessee 38019.

Our deep appreciation goes to the kind people who allowed us to photograph our projects and food in their homes.

A Beary Merry Christmas: Gerald and Jackie Record; E.A. and Janice Ostedgaard.
Christmas on the Prairie: Robert and Brenda Fellinger.
A Natural Celebration: John and Ann Hatley.
Romance and Roses: Dan and Sandra Cook.
Among the Pines and Vines: Walter and Joanne Riddick.
Reflections of the Holiday: Marvin and Nancy Haber.
Christmas Cookie Klatch: John and Kitten Weiss.
A Festive Family Dinner: Trip and Sue Larzelere.

We wish to thank the businesses that supplied some of the beautiful accessories shown in our photographs.

Brown Bag Cookie Art, Hill, New Hampshire.
Country Store Junktiques, North Little Rock, Arkansas.
Creative Critters, North Little Rock, Arkansas.
Fifth Season, Little Rock, Arkansas.
Friday's Flowers and Gifts, Little Rock, Arkansas.

We want to thank Magna IV Engravers of Little Rock, Arkansas, for their cooperative spirit, superb color reproduction, and excellent pre-press preparation.

We wish to acknowledge the excellent work of photographers Mark Mathews, Ken West, and Larry Pennington of Peerless Photography, Little Rock, Arkansas.

We extend a special thanks to Catherine Spann and her busy hands for completing so many projects for us. We also appreciate the following people for their efforts in making our projects and food extra special: Andrea Ahlen, Janet Baker, Karen Brogan, Dianna Ferguson, Sheila Jackson, Diane Kwarta, Donna McConnell, Edie Melson, Inee O'Dell, Gale O'Nale, Patricia O'Neil, Linda Pemberton, Christel Shelton, and Karen Sisco.